What About?

Navigating tough
conversations in today's world.

North Village Church: What About Sermon Series (2021)
Public Domain
Published by Amazon, Print on Demand
Graphic Designs: Mehran Poursmaeili
All Scriptures are from the NASB (New American Standard Bible, The Lockman Foundation)
Research provided by Docent Research, and used in a sermon series that was presented at North Village
Church October-November 2021.

INTRODUCTION

Welcome!

We created this booklet to help our church family engage some of the most important conversations taking place around our relationships in life.

The purpose of this booklet isn't so much to tell people what to believe, or what not to believe, but more so to acknowledge these conversations are happening, these conversations are important, and we see God's Word speaking into these conversations today.

You can look through the chapters, and quickly see these are uncomfortable chapters. It's possible some of us are thinking to ourselves, "I thought we're not supposed to talk about these things in church!"

But the reality is that these conversations are happening all around us. These conversations are coming up in school, music, movies, news, the workplace, social media, and we can all come together on Sunday morning and act like it isn't happening, or we can acknowledge they are there, they're important, and throughout this booklet we want to wrestle with how God's Word engages these conversations.

With you and for you!

TABLE OF CONTENTS

What About Women?

Today women are expected to be mothers, work outside the home, physically fit, winning personality, and a great sense of fashion. That's a lot. It's easy for women to ask the question, "Where do I fit in the local church?"

In this chapter we will focus on three sub-points:

1. Why Is This Question Important?
2. Where Do Our Culture's Answers Break Down?
3. What Does This Look Like Practically?

Why Is This Question Important?

The question around women is important, because women are important. Our culture is rallying around women with messages from the #MeToo Movement in 2017, women's salaries [1], and most recently what's our role with women's rights in other countries like Afghanistan.[2]

But God's Word has always been pro women. Did you catch that? God's Word isn't sexist, chauvinistic or oppressive toward women, and in this chapter, we want to make that as clear as possible.

> Genesis 1:26-27, "26 Then God said, "Let Us make mankind in Our image, according to Our likeness; and let them rule over the fish of the sea and over the birds of the sky and over the livestock and over all the earth, and over every crawling thing that crawls on the earth."
> 27 So God created man in His own image, in the image of God He created him; **male and female He created them**."

Somehow, and we're not sure how, but somehow the image of God is both masculine and feminine, because male and female are made in the image of God, so that God's Word is clearly pro women!

Yes, you will see verses in Scripture that will make you wonder if God's Word is pro women, and we will address some of those questions in this chapter, but generally speaking when you read Scripture as a whole you will see a progression where women are being placed in a position of honor.

---

[1] Women's Salaries. https://www.pewresearch.org/fact-tank/2021/05/25/gender-pay-gap-facts/

[2] Women's Rights In Afghanistan. https://apnews.com/article/afghanistan-cabinets-kabul-taliban-zabihullah-mujahid-be4088b24fd3c6b77bbceaf7b35c20af

It's possible there is a part of us that pushes back and thinks, "Why a progression?" Why doesn't God's Word start off with a powerful image of women from the very beginning?

It all starts in Genesis 1. In Genesis 1 we see "In the beginning God created the heavens and the earth" and in verse 27, "Male and female are made in the image of God." That's the plan. That's the dream. Everything is perfect.

But, in Genesis 3 sin enters into the story and everything falls apart, which means from Genesis 3 on - murder, death, and bloodshed is the norm of humanity.

This is difficult, but we need to imagine what life might have been like in the Old Testament. There's no system of support for women. There's no welfare program. There are no police to call for protection. There's no social structure to provide help.

There's humanity living off the land, trying to survive, and life was brutal. Therefore, when we go to the Bible and read verses where women are commanded to marry their rapist (Deuteronomy 22), or polygamy practiced by spiritual leaders (Abraham and Jacob), or Genesis 21 where a man could have numerous concubines, and our natural response today is to ask, "Why would God allow women to be treated that way?"

But we have to remember that murder, death and bloodshed of the day were common everyday challenges, and how difficult it was to simply survive in humanity.

The idea of attaching a female to a husband or a father was a means of protection in that day. In our modern lens it sounds condescending and offensive, but in the context of the day the laws in Scripture were set up to keep women safe and alive.

Keep in mind; none of that pain is what God wanted. The God of Scripture wants Genesis 1 and 2, male and female made in the image of God (1:27), be fruitful and multiply (1:28) responsibility to care for creation (2:5), all under His care and provision (2:25). That's what God wants.

But, humanity rejects God's Design (Genesis 3), and from that moment on we see the God of Scripture on mission to restore and reconcile His creation to Himself (3:15), while at the same time working in the context of murder, death, and bloodshed throughout humanity.

Where Do Our Culture's Answers Break Down?

There is a narrative in our culture right now that the Bible is oppressive toward women, and the reason that narrative exists is because you can go throughout history and pull-out references from early church leaders like Augustine, Aquinas, Luther and read comments from men about how women have very little to offer, and that's infuriating and contrary to God's Word.

All those comments are offensive, and ultimately discredit and discount the very people Jesus laid down His life. In fact, when we look at the whole of Scripture, we see a progression of women being placed in a position of honor.

Jesus interacts with women throughout scripture and constantly elevates them to positions of honor. Jesus heals women, Jesus leads through women, involves women, empowers women, and does so at a time when women had little to no value in the culture of their day. Consider these verses:

- Luke 8: The Twelve were with him, 2 and also some women who had been cured of evil spirits and diseases: Mary (called Magdalene) from whom seven demons had come out; 3 Joanna the wife of Cuza, the manager of Herod's household; Susanna; and many others. These women were helping to support them out of their own means."
- Mark 7: The woman was a Greek, born in Syrian Phoenicia. She begged Jesus to drive the demon out of her daughter.
- John 19: Near the cross of Jesus stood his mother, his mother's sister, Mary the wife of Clopas, and Mary Magdalene.
- Mark 16: Trembling and bewildered, the women went out and fled from the tomb. They said nothing to anyone, because they were afraid.
- Luke 7: Then he turned toward the woman and said to Simon, "Do you see this woman? I came into your house. You did not give me any water for my feet, but she wet my feet with her tears and wiped them with her hair.

There are some in our culture who will also tell you, "Well, Jesus might be okay, but the Apostle Paul was horrible."

But the words of the Apostle Paul are simply an extension of Jesus' Words because Paul also has women in positions of leadership throughout the New Testament, and they are used in pivotal ways to advance the kingdom of God.

Romans 16:
- · Phoebe as a deacon
- · Priscilla and Aquilla as leaders
- · Tryphena and Tryphosa who work hard

Philippians 4:
- · Euodia and Syntyche are called his fellow workers in the gospel

Proverbs 31 is another great example to see the heart of God toward women. When you read the passage on your own you see a godly woman is entrepreneurial, employs multiple people, works hard, strategic thinker, learned, cares for the poor, commands respect, loved by her family, creative, physically strong, and encourages others.

In fact, when you read Proverbs 31 we are more likely to think, "I could never live up to that calling as a woman." But you're definitely not thinking, "Scripture teaches women to get back into the kitchen."

No Proverbs 31 was light years ahead of the feminist movement, and it's because God's Word is pro women. In fact, throughout history and around the globe, the gospel hasn't oppressed women, but elevated women. [3]

Wherever you've seen the gospel flourish in countries, you've seen women in those countries flourish in education, human rights, social services, so that God's Word is the foundation of women being elevated and honored. [4]

---

[3] Amy Orr-Ewing, "Is Christianity Oppressive or Liberating to Women?" https://www.cslewisinstitute.org/webfm_send/6428

[4] Alvin J. Schmidt, "How Christianity Changed the World."

What Does This Look Like Practically?

Let's look through 1 Timothy 2 to see a practical example of what the role of women might look like in the local church.

First, were dropping into 1 Timothy 2, and we need to engage the context a little. 1 Timothy is known as a pastoral epistle. 1 Timothy is written by the Apostle Paul to a younger pastor, Timothy, who has been left in Ephesus to spiritually care for the local church.

In chapter 1 we see Timothy is discouraged, primarily from false teachers in their community, therefore the Apostle Paul admonishes Timothy to persevere, trust in Christ, and pursue peace as he navigates this tension.

In chapter 2, verses 8 and 9, we see a reference to men and women in the local church, and we see examples where we need to ask ourselves, "Is this a principle or a command?" Do you see it in verses 8 and 9?

> 1 Timothy 2:8-9, "8 Therefore I want the men in every place to pray, **lifting up holy hands**, without wrath and dissension. 9 Likewise, I want women to adorn themselves with proper clothing, modestly and discreetly, not with **braided hair** and gold or pearls or costly garments,"

We see two phrases that stand out, "lifting holy hands" and "women with braided hair" and we need to ask ourselves, "Is this a principle or a command?"

One way to know these are principles or commands is to ask if verses 8 and 9 are specific? The phrase "lifting holy hands" is somewhat general. In fact, it's a figure of speech to capture one's posture in worship.

In addition, "braided hair" isn't offensive to God, but more so the Apostle Paul is giving us a principle not to rely on physical appearances. Let's keep reading.

> 1 Timothy 2:10-11, "10 but rather by means of **good works**, as is proper for women making a claim to godliness. 11 A woman must **quietly** receive instruction with entire **submissiveness**."

What do these verses mean? At first glance these verses could lead us to slam the Bible shut and reject anything it has to offer, but first we need to be aware of our personal bias when we read this verse as a 21st Century American.

We have been influenced by our culture. We, as a people, are a product of the Civil Rights Movement, Suffrage, #MeToo, movies, songs, literature that are fighting for women's rights, which is great. Therefore, whether we like it or not, we are going to read those verses with a bias that makes it easy for us to get triggered, so we need to go slow.

Second, the Apostle Paul, who is often villianized in some circles, is calling women to "good works" in verse 10. In fact, he is admonishing women to not get too swept up in physical appearances, at a time when almost every culture would have valued women for their physical appearances, but instead the Apostle Paul presses women into living meaningful lives of good works. [5]

---

[5] In her commentary on 1 Peter, Karen Jobes summarizes some of the beauty codes to which women were subjected in the first century:

- For Xenophon, a woman adorns the world by the daily practice of the virtues (Xenophon, *Oeconomicus*, 7.43).
- For Aristotle, a woman's self-control in all she does and her inclination toward an honorable and well-ordered life with patience and gentleness are her true beauties (Aristotle, *Oeconomica* 3.1).
- Conversely, outward adornments were often perceived as instruments of seduction (Philo, *On the Virtues*, 7.39; Plutarch, *Advice*, para. 30) and a woman's use of cosmetics was viewed as an attempt to deceive; both were unnecessary if a woman stayed at home (Xenophon, *Oeconomicus*, 10.2)."

And, then third, in verse 11 we tend not to be able to take our eyes off the word "submissiveness," but we need to see that the Apostle Paul is admonishing women to good works (10) and learning, which again, would have been counter cultural for women in the first century.

In the Roman world in the first century, women were thought to be intellectually second-class.[6] It was widely accepted that females were mentally inferior, so that most learning systems were designed for men, not women, but the Apostle Paul is encouraging women to learn.

Now, yes, verse 11 also includes two phrases that are uncomfortable; "learn quietly" and "submission" and I am sure that many of us have images of women being oppressed, and as a result we have a natural impulse that pushes back but lean in with us for just a second.

The admonition to "learn quietly" is simply to pursue a quiet and peaceful life. It isn't an admonition to never speak unless spoken to, get back in the kitchen, or sit down and be quiet.

In fact, this same admonition of "learn quietly" is given to Timothy in verse 2 to lead a quiet and peaceful life, because of all the false teaching, gossip, and slander that is taking place in their culture.

---

[6] Alvin J. Schmidt, "How Christianity Changed the World." The letter from the year 1 B.C.E from Hilarion to his pregnant wife Alis (Note the concern and affection for his wife) "Know that I am still in Alexandria. And do not worry if they all come back and I remain in Alexandria. I ask and beg you to take good care of our baby son, and as soon as I receive payment I shall send it up to you. If you are delivered of a child [before I come home], if it is a boy keep it, if a girl discard it. You have sent me word, "Don't forget me." How can I forget you. I beg you not to worry.

When it comes to the word "submission" it is a word that is difficult for us to read today because it is a word that has a negative connotation. But we need to remember when we see "submission" in Scripture, our ultimate submission is to the God of Scripture where men and women are called to submit to God and love one another.

Therefore, with this understanding in mind, there is no concept of submission in Scripture that is intended to be abusive, heavy handed, or toxic in any capacity.

And the best picture of submission in Scripture is captured in the Trinity between the Father, Son and Spirit as they mutually submit to one another, so that submission isn't a connotation of value, but order as we all submit to the Lord. Let's keep reading. Let's look at verse 12:

> 1 Timothy 12, "12 But I do not allow a woman to teach or exercise authority over a man, but to remain quiet."

Now, verse 12 is a verse that can trigger some emotions. I want to make sure we take a minute to acknowledge our bias and lean into God's Word.

The context of verse 12 doesn't apply to all women and all men at all times. The idea that Scripture teaches all women to stay home, be quiet and make babies is offensive because we see countless examples of women in Scripture leading and influencing in all areas of life.

The context of verse 12 is specifically in the local church, and specifically at the elder level, because again, false teaching is taking place in the culture, and the elder is where spiritual authority and teaching is taking place so as to guard the spiritual health of the local church.

Therefore, when you turn the page to chapter 3 in 1 Timothy, we see this position of influence isn't given to all men because they are male, but it is given to specific men who embody the characteristics of an elder described in 1 Timothy 3 to shepherd the flock.

This is the model that we follow at North Village Church, and the natural pushback to that response is what we discussed earlier in verses 8 and 9 which is, "Isn't this just cultural? Isn't this outdated? Does this really apply to today?" Great question. Look at verses 13-15:

> 1 Timothy 2:13-15, "13 For it was Adam who was first created, and then Eve. 14 And it was not Adam who was deceived, but the woman being deceived, fell into transgression. 15 But women will be preserved through the bearing of children if they continue in faith and love and sanctity with self-restraint."

In verse 13 the Apostle Paul grounds this instruction not in culture of the day, but in creation, and points us back to Genesis 1-2 where Adam is given "spiritual responsibility," and Eve is invited to be a "suitable helper."

Therefore, in the context of North Village Church, we want women influencing our church family at all levels, except the role of the elder.

We have women speaking into the plans of our church family every year. We have women leading us in worship, leading our ministry teams, leading out in groups and breakout sessions, and it's because our church family needs spiritual women, mothers, and sisters reflected in the life of our church.

It's possible that a person might be saying to themselves, "I don't believe this, or I can't believe this" and that's okay. We're not trying to tell people what to believe, but what would be most important for all of us to understand is that our value in life and our value in the local church doesn't come from possessing one particular title, or serving in one particular ministry, but our value and identity comes from being a son and a daughter in Christ, who came at great cost to Himself to live for you, die for you, and rise for you.

Jesus is the One who died for you. Jesus is the One who came for you. Jesus is the One who sends us out to proclaim His name so that as many as possible might be reconciled to Him.

Reflective Questions:
1. How have our current cultural events shaped how you read Genesis 2?
2. What about other Scriptures where we see women in leadership roles?

Additional Resources:
- Women in the Church by Kostenberger.
- Two Views on Women in Ministry by Gundry.
- 5 Evidences of Complementarian Gender Roles in Genesis 1-2 by Denny Burk.
- Head to Head about 1 Corinthians 11:3–16 by Claire Smith.

What About Abortion?

Abortion is a conversation that reaches into areas of science, biology, theology, ethics, and politics, and that makes this conversation complicated, but this conversation is also incredibly personal.

In this chapter we will focus on three sub-points:

1. Define The Conversation.
2. How Does God's Word Engage The Conversation?
3. How Do We Respond Practically?

1. Define The Conversation.

In order to get into the details of the conversation, we do need to begin with some basic description of abortion to make sure we are all on the same page.

Abortion is the act by which the fetus is prematurely exited from the uterus, which ends the pregnancy, and results in the death of the fetus.

The reason this happens could be a miscarriage, which is involuntary and unplanned, but when it is voluntary and planned it is technically termed an induced abortion.

The conversation we are discussing in this chapter is not an unplanned miscarriage, but a planned process with a medical professional with the intent of removing the fetus from the uterus to terminate the pregnancy.

While we can find examples of abortive practices throughout history, the most notable is Roe. v Wade in 1973 when the United States Supreme Court ruled that the Constitution protects a pregnant woman's liberty to choose to have an abortion.

There are several means by which an abortion can take place. In the first 72 hours of pregnancy a woman can use a pill known as "Morning After Pill" which you can pick up at Walgreens pharmacy to terminate the pregnancy.

In the first 10-weeks of pregnancy a woman can use an "Abortion Pill" - that you have to get through a medical professional to terminate the pregnancy - which will induce cramping and an emptying of the uterus.

Outside of 10 weeks a woman needs to go through the process of a surgical abortion, which is done with anesthesia, and a tube empties the uterus. And beyond 14 weeks forceps are used to insert a tube combined with medical tools to forcefully remove the fetus.

Around the world there are 125,000 abortions every day. [7] In the United States, Guttmacher, a pro-abortion research group, stated 862,320 surgical abortions were performed in 2017. [8] Just to give contrast, 679K have died from Covid in the last year and a half. [9]

The most common reason women are giving for abortions today are to postpone childbearing, and the second is for socio-economic concerns which include disruption of education or employment, lack of support from the father, desire to provide for existing children, and unemployment.[10]

We could take time to critique arguments around when life begins, and perhaps in the 1980's and 1990's that would have been a viable discussion, but due to the advancement in technology we are seeing more and more people, on both sides of the argument, conclude that life begins at conception.

Writing for *The Atlantic*, Caitlin Flannigan in 2019 acknowledges the fetus as a human being because of the 3D Imaging we have available today. (Picture provided of a 20-week fetus as an example on the next page.)

"The first time I saw one of the new 3-D ultrasounds of a fetus in utero, I wasn't entirely sure what I was looking at. It wasn't anything like the black-and-white images I was used to seeing…. For a long time, these images made me anxious.

---

[7] Number of abortions around the world. https://www.worldometers.info/abortions/

[8] Number of abortions in the United States. https://www.guttmacher.org/fact-sheet/induced-abortion-united-states#

[9] Number based on October 2021.

[10] Reason for abortions. https://www.guttmacher.org/journals/psrh/2005/reasons-us-women-have-abortions-quantitative-and-qualitative-perspectives

They are proof that what grows within a pregnant woman's body is a human being, living and unfolding according to a timetable that has existed as long as we have. Obviously, it would take a profound act of violence to remove him from his quiet world and destroy him."

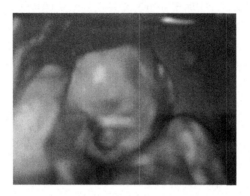

Probably the most influential arguments for abortion in our culture today are grounded in women having the same rights as men.

The assumption is that if men can walk away from a pregnancy, then women should be able to walk away from a pregnancy, which makes sense on some level. But why should babies suffer so that men and women can exercise sexual freedom?

In fact, in the context of abortion, the unborn baby suffers, the woman who goes through the abortion suffers trauma and pain that is rarely talked about, and yet still today the man walks away with minimal cost. How is that a win for women?

2. How Does God's Word Engage The Conversation?

Now, lets talk about God's Word. How does a follower of Jesus respond to this conversation? Before we read God's Word, we want to acknowledge the potential for shame and guilt to be layered in this conversation.

Our emotions might be sensitive because a friend or family member has experienced an abortion. Or it might difficult because of our personal experience. Or it might be challenging because we worked in an abortion clinic.

Either way, over the last 50 years we can be confident this conversation isn't just an academic subject, but it is a personal subject. Therefore, as we transition to God's Word, we need to remember we are transition to God's Word with a great measure of grace. Let's read Psalm 139:13-18:

139:13-18, "13 For You formed my inward parts; you wove me in my mother's womb. 14 I will give thanks to You, for I am fearfully and wonderfully made; wonderful are Your works, and my soul knows it very well. 15 My frame was not hidden from You, when I was made in secret, and skillfully wrought in the depths of the earth; 16 Your eyes have seen my unformed substance; and in Your book were all written the days that were ordained for me, when as yet there was not one of them. 17 How precious also are Your thoughts to me, O God! How vast is the sum of them! 18 If I should count them, they would outnumber the sand. When I awake, I am still with You."

The psalms in general are a collection of poetical writings about the God of Scripture. Psalm 139 specifically addresses the attributes and characteristics of God, so when you read Psalm 139 on your own, you will see the first 12 verses focus on the all-knowing attributes of God.

In verses 13-18 we see the God of Scripture is involved even in our prenatal development. He is sovereign over life, both inside the womb and outside the womb, and until we are face-to-face with Him in eternity.

In addition, note the tender words of our Heavenly Father through the psalm. There is intimacy. There is relationship. There is intentionality. There is purpose.

Those two words "inward parts" literally mean kidneys, referring to a person's vital organs, so that something like that of a supernatural potter and the clay is taking place inside the womb of the mother. Consider the 3-D image again:

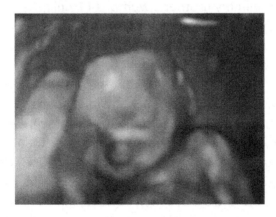

When you look at the face of the baby it looks like a thumb is coming across the face much like a sculptor's thumb would come across a piece of clay as the piece is molded together.

It's likely just a glitch on the screen, but that glitch is also a reminder of what Psalm 139 is teaching, which is the God of Scripture knows us inside and out, beginning to end, and the God of Scripture leaves His fingerprints all over us.

The fingerprints of God on humanity are a dominant theme throughout Scripture, which means our value in humanity isn't because of our titles, finances, strength or beauty, but our value is because the fingerprints of His glory are all over humanity. And as a follower of Jesus, this shapes how we see all of humanity.

There is a critique of the pro-life view that followers of Jesus are very passionate about pre-birth, but tend to be less interested in post-birth, and as followers of Jesus we need to own this critique. [11]

Scripture makes it clear that followers of Jesus are to care for women, orphans, and widows (James 1:27). Therefore, as a follower of Jesus we want to model a pattern of not only adoption, but also foster care, caring for the homeless, caring for the elderly, the sick, the vulnerable, and in all areas to care for those who are hurting, because we want to be passionate for life at every level, because Jesus is passionate for life at every level.

Jesus is the One who spoke life into existence. Jesus is the One who took on flesh, born as a baby. Jesus is the One who comes for the wounded, oppressed, sick, and Jesus is the One who takes our flaws and failures at the cross so that we might have life in Him.

---

[11] We Can't Be Pro-Life If We're Not Anti-Poverty by Katie McCoy. January 4, 2017. https://www.texanonline.net/articles/special-reports/we-cant-be-pro-life-if-were-not-anti-poverty/

3. **How Do We Respond Practically?**

Advocating for life might be unpopular in our culture today, but as followers of Jesus, we want to be a voice for the voiceless. Therefore, these are just a few practical ways to respond:

We pray. There is power in prayer. We want to intercede on behalf of the poor, needy, hurting and overwhelmed. We want to pray that our hearts would be softened to those who are hurting. We want to pray that the Lord would open our eyes to ways we can help.

We want to educate ourselves. There are resources online. There are books to read. There are agencies that North Village Church partner with called The Source here in Austin, and it is too easy not be well informed.

We can celebrate life. At North Village Church we love seeing children run around after the worship service on a Sunday morning. We love talking about the joy of parenthood. We love seeing moms get pregnant and celebrate their pregnancy.

We are saddened when followers of Jesus mock the idea of bringing children into this world. Children are a gift (Psalm 123:7). Life is beautiful and needs to be celebrated.

We can support women. We want to make it easy to have children. We want to celebrate marriage. We want to celebrate weddings. We want to celebrate pregnancies, so that women are excited to have children.

We can support fathers. It is far too easy for a man to put the responsibility of pregnancy on the woman. Therefore, we want to educate our men, we want to encourage our men, and when we see our men working hard to bring life into this world, then we want to support them and encourage them.

We can share the 3 Circles Gospel Presentation. We want to look around so that we can point people to Jesus. The darkness of abortion can only be solved by the light of Christ, and it is His gospel that is powerful to save. [12]

We want to be involved politically. Today this conversation is politically divisive, but it wasn't always.

Even 15 years ago you would see a robust pro-life wing of the Democratic Party. [13] Therefore, we must pray for the Lord to raise up men and women who care about life before birth, and after birth.

We want men and women who will welcome refugees, stand against racism, model people of character and integrity, and care for the life of an unborn child.

We want to embody a posture of humility. A person's moral clarity doesn't give them the right to be arrogant, harsh, and insensitive to others. Might the people around us find God's people to be strong, but also gracious, kind, tender and empathetic.

We want to take action. It can't be enough to just land on a philosophical view, but we must all look for ways to provide practical support on some level (a meal, gift, time, foster, adopt) in the act of new life coming into this world.

---

[12] The 3 Circles Gospel Presentation October 3, 2017.
https://www.youtube.com/watch?v=5W8ynRMr59k

[13] https://www.democratsforlife.org/

Closing Thoughts

For those who have had an abortion, or know someone who has had an abortion, then you know there are layers of despair, regret, sorrow, shame, and we want you to know there is hope for you today.

There is hope for the broken-hearted, hope for the medical practitioner, hope for the boyfriend or husband who didn't say anything, because the good news of Jesus is available to all people.

We have all chosen death, and yet our Heavenly Father didn't give up. He pursued us, loves us and extends compassion to us by Jesus taking our sin at the cross.

Through faith in Jesus our guilt has been paid. Our hearts can be made clean. Please don't sit in any despair but see this as an opportunity to turn to Jesus and find living hope.

Reflective Questions:
1. How has your experience with abortion personally shaped how you engage this conversation today?
2. What does it look like practically for you to celebrate life and serve children?

Additional Resources:
- Counter Culture by David Platt.
- 5 Ways to Start a Conversation With a Woman Considering Abortion by Katie McCoy.

What About People Who Haven't Heard About Jesus?

What does the Bible say about people who are Muslim, Mormon, Buddhist, Hindu, or atheist? What about the person who lives in the jungle and never has contact with anyone?   How do we engage that conversation today?

In this chapter we will focus on three sub-points:

1.   Define The Conversation.
2.   What Are The Objections?
3.   How Does God's Word Respond?

1. Define The Conversation.

As we step into this conversation, we need to acknowledge this isn't a hypothetical conversation.

We are talking about real people, real lives, for eternity. Therefore, we want to be clear in this conversation. But we also want to be sensitive and gentle when we talk about this conversation.

This is the challenge in all these conversations of our day. We don't want to be so clear that we are hurtful, but we don't want to be so gentle that we are ambiguous. Therefore, let's begin with a statement:

Scripture is clear-only upon hearing the name of Jesus, and responding in faith and repentance, can we be reconciled to the God of Scripture and spend eternity with Him.

There are many verses we could read, but here are a few to consider:

John 14:6, "Jesus said to him, "I am the way, and the truth, and the life; no one comes to the Father but through Me."

Acts 4:12, "And there is salvation in no one else; for there is no other name under heaven that has been given among men by which we must be saved."

1 John 5:12, "He who has the Son has the life; he who does not have the Son of God does not have the life."

John 3:18, "He who believes in Him is not judged; he who does not believe has been judged already, because he has not believed in the name of the only begotten Son of God."

It is common for people to see those verses and say, "Yes, but Jesus was about love, gentleness, patience, sympathy, and I don't think Jesus will hold us accountable for something someone has never heard."

And to be clear, Jesus is loving, gentle, patient, and sympathetic, but we must also see Jesus makes radical statements about the importance of His role in humanity and they are statements of superiority.

John 11: I am the resurrection and the life.

Notice Jesus doesn't say, "My life points to the resurrection, I am a symbol of resurrection." But Jesus is clear, "I am the resurrection."

Mark 2: I am the Lord of the Sabbath.

In Mark 2 Jesus heals a man on the Sabbath and the religious leaders say, "You shouldn't be working on the Sabbath."

Again, Jesus doesn't say, "I point to the Sabbath, I model the Sabbath, I encourage people to take Sabbaths." No, Jesus says, "I am the source and author of the eternal Sabbath rest."

Mark 11: I am rest.

In Mark 11, when Jesus speaks of rest, He doesn't reference others, He doesn't encourage other books, He doesn't point to other prophets, but instead Jesus says, "Come to me, all who are weary and heavy-laden, and I will give you rest.

In fact, if you read about Jesus' life in Matthew, Mark, Luke, and John you will see there is never a discourse where Jesus embraces ambiguity.

Instead, Jesus is always challenging, always pushing, always pointing people to either reject Him, or follow Him and worship Him as Lord, so that you could really take the life of Jesus and break His life down into four categories.

1. Jesus' Power: There is no other religious leader in history who did what Jesus did. Miracles over nature, over life, over sickness, and then personally conquering death in the resurrection and appearing to over 500 people over 40 days. Every other religious leader is dead. Jesus is alive. (Matthew 8:23-27, Luke 7:11-18, Matthew 8:5-13, 1 Corinthians 15)

2. Jesus' Predicted: 100's of years before Jesus is born, we see promises of what Jesus would look like, where He would be born, when He would be born, so much so that other people were trying to fake Jesus' life so that they would look like the Savior. But Jesus is the only one who fulfilled them all. (Isaiah 7:14, 2 Samuel 7:12, Hosea 11:1, Micah 5:2)

3. Jesus' Preaching: Not only did Jesus do the miraculous, but His teaching was miraculous. No other religious leader has talked the way Jesus talked. Every other religious leader tells us what to do. Jesus tells us what He would do, and then He did it. (Matthew 16:21-28 and Mark 9:30-32)

4. Jesus' Perfection: No other religious leader has lived like Jesus. Jesus was perfect in every way. Others make claims that point us to God, but Jesus told us He was and is God. (Luke 23:47, John 19:4, John 1:1)

This is why we can start off the chapter with this singular statement:

> Scripture is clear-only upon hearing the name of Jesus, and responding in faith and repentance, can we be reconciled to the God of Scripture and spend eternity with Him.

We know this is hard to hear, we know this is controversial in our culture today, and we know there is a layer in us that wants to push back and say, "But what about the millions and millions of innocent people all over the world?"

And we will touch on that objection in this chapter in a minute, but when we say to ourselves, or to others phrases like, "We are all God's Children, God knows our heart, all faiths are the same" then you need to know we are rejecting God's Word and we are calling Jesus a liar, because Scripture is clear-only upon hearing the name of Jesus, and responding in faith and repentance, can we be reconciled to the God of Scripture and spend eternity with Him.

2. What are the objections?

First, the primary objection a person might give is, "Who cares?" Who cares about Jesus? Who cares about eternity? Why does this conversation even matter?

The reason this conversation matters is because there is pain and suffering in this world. Pain and suffering aren't something we can ignore.

We don't get to choose if there is pain and suffering in this world. There just is pain and suffering, and as human beings we must figure out a way to navigate the pain and suffering of our day.

This chapter is making the argument that Jesus is the best answer to help us navigate the pain and suffering in this world! [14]

Jesus doesn't respond to our pain and suffering by saying, "Pain and suffering isn't real, just meditate." Jesus doesn't say, "Do all these things to overcome pain and suffering." Jesus doesn't say, "Just love one another and pain and suffering will go away."

But instead, Jesus says, "I will take your pain and suffering at the cross and defeat it for eternity" so that we can have living, eternal hope in Him today.

Second, people will say, "Isn't it better to just say, 'All faiths are basically the same?'" It sounds more inclusive. It sounds more accepting.

But do you know how offensive it is to walk up to any faith system of the day and say, "Your faith is basically like Buddhism, Islam, Christianity, and every other faith system of the day. It's not very unique. It's not that different."

---

[14] Rebecca Pippert, *Hope Has Its Reasons.* (Harper 1990), Chapter 4, "What Kind of God Gets Angry?"

In a culture that values tolerance and acceptance, you need to know that response is very offensive. And the statement "all faiths are basically the same" is an arrogant statement draped in humility. [15]

It is a statement that sounds humble and accepting, while at the same time making a dogmatic statement "all faiths are the same." Please don't say that to people. It's rude. [16]

Third, and last, people will say, "But surely God will give a special pass at some point. What about those millions and millions of people who never hear about Jesus? How can people be held responsible if they've never heard?"

Here's the problem, if never hearing the gospel was a means by which we get an exemption, then we should never share the gospel.

If that statement were true then we should put the gospel in a box, lock it up and hide it away forever so that humanity can always claim that exemption. But instead, in the life of Jesus and the disciples, we see the exact opposite.

We see them tirelessly taking the name of Jesus around the known world. We see them sacrificing their lives, sacrificing comforts so that as many as possible might hear the name of Jesus and be reconciled to God.

3. How Does God's Word Respond?

Let's look at Romans 1:18-25. Romans is written by the Apostle Paul, and in the beginning of chapter 1 we see the

---

[15] Kathryn Tanner, "Respect for Other Religions: A Christian Antidote for Colonialist Discourse," *Modern Theology* 9 (1993), 2.

[16] Newbigin, *The Gospel in a Pluralist Society*, 9-10.

Apostle Paul in awe of the life, death, and resurrection of Jesus. In verse 18 the Apostle Paul begins to explain why Jesus is so important.

> Romans 1:18, "18 For the **wrath of God** is revealed from heaven against all ungodliness and unrighteousness of men who **suppress the truth** in unrighteousness"

When we see the phrase "wrath of God" that makes us uncomfortable, but you need to know the God of Scripture is always fair.

1 Peter 1:17 says our Heavenly Father is impartial in His judgment. Romans 2:11 says our God shows no partiality. None of us are comfortable with God's judgment, but the answer isn't indifference and a removal of judgment. If so, evil and wickedness would go on for eternity.

No, our greatest hope is that the wickedness of humanity will be held accountable, and we can take great comfort that when the accountability takes place, the God of Scripture will be fair in His judgment.

Second, the word "suppress" means all of humanity knows God, and literally "pushes the knowledge of God out of our lives."

This means the tribesman in the darkest jungles knows God. The middle school student at Murchison Middle School knows God, and both push the knowledge of God out of their lives. Look at verses 19-20:

> Romans 1:19-20, "19 because that which is known about God is evident within them; for God made it evident to them. 20 For since the creation of the world His **invisible**

attributes, His **eternal power** and **divine nature**, have been clearly seen, being understood through what has been made, so that they are without excuse."

How does all of humanity throughout all of history "know God" and "suppress the knowledge of God?" We do it through ignoring God's "invisible attributes, eternal power and divine nature" revealed in creation.

This doesn't mean every person in history knows about Sunday morning worship at North Village Church, but verses 19-20 are teaching that every person in history knows deep inside of themselves that there is the divine Creator God, because verse 19, "that which is known about God is evident to them, because God made it evident to them" and we push the knowledge of God out of our lives.

It's like if we go to the dentist and the dentist says we have a cavity, and we say to ourselves, "I don't want to think about that right now."

Or, we go to school and the teacher says, "We have a test on Monday" and we think to ourselves, "I don't want to think about that right now."

It is as though humanity sees the complexity of muscle tissue, the expanse of stars, planets, and galaxies, the beauty of mountains, land and sea, and concludes, "Oh, obviously those detailed, intelligently designed, beautiful things spontaneously sprung into existence."

So, first, when we wrestle with this question, we need to be clear, "God Is Always Fair" (18). Second, we need to be clear, "All People Know There Is A God" (19-20). Third, we need to be clear, "All People Reject God" (21). Look at verse 21:

Romans 1:21, "21 For even though they knew God, they **did not honor Him** as God or give thanks, but they became futile in their speculations, and their foolish heart was darkened."

Romans 3 says we have all fallen short of the glory of God. Ephesians 2 teaches that we are dead in our sin. Genesis 3 teaches us we are cast from His presence. John 8

teaches us we are spiritually blind, so that in our state of spiritual death and darkness we not only suppress and reject, but we also exchange. Look at verses 22-23:

Romans 1:22-23, "22 Professing to be wise, they became fools, 23 and **exchanged** the glory of the incorruptible God for an image in the form of corruptible man and of birds and four-footed animals and crawling creatures."

Do you see the problem in humanity isn't ignorance? The problem in humanity isn't an opportunity. In Romans 1 we see humanity "knows there is a divine Creator" at the core of our soul, and this is important. We simply exchange our interests to something else.

The bible calls those things idols, but today we call them hobbies. Have you noticed we don't just eat food, we worship food? We don't just work a job; we worship our career. We don't just fall in love, we become stalkers. We don't just make some money, we worship money because we suppress, reject, and exchange.

Therefore, when we talk about this question, we need to remember God is always fair (18). Second, all people know there is a God (19-20). Third, all people reject Him (21). Fourth, we not only reject, but we also exchange

(22-23), so that the fifth take-away is that there are no innocent people.

We always think to ourselves, "What about the innocent people of the world?" But the word "innocent" is so important because there are no innocent people in the world. You know that's true.

If people are "innocent" then those people will spend eternity with Jesus, but none of us are innocent. Therefore, it doesn't matter what country you live in, or what point in history we are born because we can be confident there are no innocent people in the world.

So, when we ask the question, "What happens to people who never believe in Jesus?" The answer is they perish. This is why Jesus is so important.

Jesus is the creator of all things (Colossians 1), and Jesus sees His creation not only rejecting Him, but giving its adoration to man-made idols, and yet His response is to step out of the heavens, take on flesh, go through the humility of being put to death at the cross and conquer death in the resurrection so that whosoever might believe in Him will find life, and life abundantly. That's the gospel.

We hope you hear some urgency in this conversation. There is urgency to respond. There is urgency to believe in Jesus today.

You don't have to attend a local church. You don't have to vote a particular way. You don't have to dress a certain way. But you do need to believe in Jesus today.

Romans 10:9 teaches us to confess with our mouth that Jesus is Lord and believe in our heart that Jesus resurrected from the dead and you will be saved.

If anyone has never turned to Jesus and committed their life to Him, do that today!

Reflective Questions:
1. How would you respond if someone asked you, "What about people who haven't heard about Jesus?"
2. How does pain and suffering in our world today shape how we respond to this question today?

Additional Resources:
- The Reason for God by Timothy Keller.

What About Sex Before Marriage?

It's possible the subject of this chapter might seem outdated because sex is so widely accepted in our culture today, but God's Word is going to cast a completely different understanding of sex than what we see in our culture today.

In this chapter we will focus on three sub-points:

1. Why Do We Drift Toward Sex?
2. What About Marriage?
3. How Does God's Word Respond?

1. Why Do We Drift Toward Sex?

Let's begin with a reminder of why the good news of Jesus is such good news. It is likely that every person who reads these words will be coming from a variety of sexual experiences. Therefore, we need to be reminded that the God of Scripture isn't shocked by our sexual experiences.

All of us have fallen short sexually. Jesus knows our thoughts. Jesus knows the secret things we have done, or have been done to us, things we hope nobody ever finds out, so we need to remember the gospel is that Jesus moves toward us in this conversation.

Jesus has come to bring healing. Jesus has come to bring forgiveness. Jesus has come to take our sexual shortcomings upon Himself and put them to death at the cross so that we might be made clean.

First, when we talk about sex, we need to make sure we are all on the same page. When we talk about sex, we are talking about sex in the broadest sense.

We are talking about sex between two people in a bed under the covers. We are talking about oral sex. We are talking about solo-sex, or masturbation with pornographic materials. And we are talking about any kind of sex and everything in between.

Second, when our culture talks about sex, our culture rallies around three values when it comes to sex:

1. One may not **criticize** someone's sexual choices.
2. One may not **coerce** or cause harm to others.
3. One may not engage in sexual relationships without **consent**. [17]

As a result, our culture tries to present sex as something that is just a physical act between two consenting people,

---

[17] See Dale S. Kuehne, *Sex and the iWorld: Rethinking Relationships beyond an Age of Individualism.*

and as long as nobody gets hurt, anything goes. But this is a lie, and we want to draw out how this is a lie philosophically and biologically.

First, it is a lie philosophically. The idea of separating the mind, body and soul so that our bodies are meaningless inanimate objects is foolish. It's a great marketing ad to get people to vacation in Las Vegas, but "What happens in Vegas doesn't stay in Vegas."

What do we tell children when they are full of energy? We tell them to go outside and run off that energy. We tell them to exert physical exercise. What do we tell people when people are stressed out? We tell them to exert physical exercise.

Why? Because our physical body affects our emotions, but somehow, we think we can engage in sexual activity / physical activity and tell ourselves, "It's just physical." It's silly.

Second, it is a lie biologically. We know when we participate in sexual activity (any type of sexual activity I referenced earlier) we release oxytocin, a chemical associated with relational bonding, so that it is biologically impossible to do sexual things with our bodies and that not affect us. [18]

Psychologists refer to this relational bonding as "sex glue" and when we experience sexual release with people, or two-dimensional objects through masturbation and pornography, we are doing two disorienting things to ourselves. [19]

---

[18] Christian Smith, Lost, 180.

[19] What Is the Link Between Oxytocin and Love?
https://www.medicalnewstoday.com/articles/275795

One, we are creating "sex glue connections" with those people or objects (which is what creates fetishes), and then second, we are training ourselves to have shallow relationships every time we rip that "sex glue" apart. [20]

As a result, the average person goes through life with a myriad of sexual experiences, and we then tell ourselves "We're fine, it's what everyone is doing."

Then we casually stumble into a marriage, and when the marriage starts to get difficult, we wonder to ourselves, "What happened? Why is this relationship so difficult?"

But of course, our relationships are going to be difficult. We have been living a life of start / stop sexual experiences and training ourselves to keep shallow relationships.

It doesn't mean there is no hope. Jesus has come to bring hope, but it would be naïve to think, "What I do with my body is just physical and doesn't affect me," because that's a lie.

2.   What About Marriage?

When we talk about marriage, we need to acknowledge that our culture has a mixed relationship with marriage in general.

- We love engagements and weddings.
- We love shows like the Bachelor and Bachelorette.
- We love celebrity marriages.
- 2 billion watched the wedding of Harry and Meghan.
- We love movies and songs about love and marriage.
- 4,145,237 people got married in the U.S. in 2017

---

[20] Definition of oxytocin. https://www.psychologytoday.com/us/basics/oxytocin

But we also have some things about marriage that we are not very fond of:

- We've watered down a biblical idea of marriage.
- Most have seen our parents go through a divorce.
- We have friends that are chronically unhappy in marriage.
- We receive conflicting messages about how to fix our marriages, or if we should even try.

As a result, we have this mixed messaging taking place in our culture around marriage. [21] In general, we don't think of marriage as a lifetime commitment, but instead marriage is kind of a glorified dating experiment that we exit quickly when the relationship gets difficult.

But marriage is a gift given to humanity in the earliest pages of Scripture. Consider Genesis 2:18:

Genesis 2:18, "18 Then the Lord God said, "**It is not good for the man to be alone**; I will make him a helper suitable for him."

This phrase, "It is not good for man to be alone" should jump off the page because up to this point everything God has done in Genesis 1-2 has been, "Good." God creates light, "Good." God creates land, "Good." God creates life, "Good". But now, in verse 18, Scripture says, "It is not good" because in verse 18 the God of Scripture is introducing the gift of marriage.

[21] Hugo Schwyzer, "How Marital Infidelity Became America's Last Sexual Taboo," The Atlantic, May 29, 2013.
https://www.theatlantic.com/sexes/archive/2013/05/how-marital-infidelity-became-americas-last-sexual-taboo/276341/

In addition, notice at the end of verse 18 that it says, "I will make him a helper suitable for him." Verse 18 is teaching us what the role of a wife looks like in marriage.

When we see the words like "Helper" and "Suitable" it could make our eyes start twitching because it is language that sounds oppressive toward women. But we know Genesis 1 says, "Male and female are made in the image of God," so this word "Helper" can't mean women are inferior.

In fact, this word "Helper," in the original language, is a word of power. This word "Helper" has a connotation of military reinforcements, like, "Oh no, get the helper!"

This word "Helper" is the same word used of "God as our helper" in Psalm 54. This is the same word that Jesus assigns to the Holy Spirit as "Our Helper" so that in verse 18 the God of Scripture is looking at Adam and saying, "I am going to send him the helper."

And she's not just any old "helper." She's a "suitable helper." Do you see that word in verse 18? The word "suitable" means she's a complimentary helper.

The God of Scripture could have brought in an animal. He could have brought in another man. But the gift of marriage is set apart to be one man, one woman, so that they might compliment one another. Look at verses 19-20 to see the role of the husband:

Genesis 2:19-20, "19 And out of the ground the Lord God formed every animal of the field and every bird of the sky, and brought them **to the man to see what he would call them**; and whatever the man called a living creature, that was its name. 20 The man gave names to all the livestock, and to the birds of the sky, and to every animal of the field, but for Adam there was not found a helper suitable for him."

In verse 18 we see the divine role of a wife in marriage, and in verses 19-20 we see the divine role of a husband in marriage as Adam is set apart to be a spiritual leader.

Earlier, in verse 15, you see Adam given responsibility to care for the garden. In verse 16 you see God speaking directly to Adam to obey God and enjoy God, so that in Genesis 2 we see the divine role of a husband in marriage as a spiritual leader in marriage.

Now, this language of "spiritual leader" doesn't mean the husband's the boss. It doesn't mean the husbands more important. It doesn't mean the husband gets what he wants.

The language of "spiritual leader" means someone needs to be responsible for the spiritual health of the marriage, and the God of Scripture has given that responsibility to the husband.

This doesn't mean everyone needs to get married, but God's Word makes it clear that marriage is important, and marriage should be held in high honor (Hebrews 13:4).

3. How Does God's Word Respond?

As mentioned earlier, our culture rallies around three values when it comes to sex:

1. One may not **criticize** someone's sexual choices.
2. One may not **coerce** or cause harm to others.

45

3. One may not engage in sexual relationships without **consent**. [22]

God's Word affirms points 2 and 3, but God's Word absolutely speaks into our sexual and our marital life. Therefore, let's begin by looking at the biblical foundation of marriage in Song of Solomon. Look at verses 2:1-3:

> Song of Solomon 2:1-3, "I am the rose of Sharon, the lily of the valleys." 2 "Like a lily among the thorns, so is my darling among the maidens." 3 "Like an apple tree among the trees of the forest, so is my beloved among the young men. In his shade I took great delight and sat down, and his fruit was sweet to my taste."

Song of Solomon is poetic language so it can be difficult to follow. The first verse is the woman speaking as she highlights how beautiful she sees herself in the context of the relationship.

The second verse is Solomon highlighting her beauty, and the third verse it is the woman speaking of her love for Solomon, "Like an apple tree among the forest," meaning Solomon stands out in a crowd.

In verse 3 we see she takes great delight in his shade, which is a reminder of his protection. And we're not exactly sure what the phrase "fruit being sweet to the taste," but it is clear there is some romantic language being used.

Now, at this point in the relationship, these two aren't married, but they are romantically interested in one another. And this is important to clarify because sometimes

---

[22] See Dale S. Kuehne, Sex and the iWorld: Rethinking Relationships beyond an Age of Individualism.

in the local church sex has been presented as gross, shame or improper. But God's Word is absolutely the path toward sex-positivity.

In fact, you won't find anyone more positive about sex than the One who created sex. This is especially true for women because in Song of Solomon the woman, not the man, is the dominant voice through the poetical language.

It is the woman who seeks, pursues, initiates, and boldly exclaims her physical attraction, and this is radical considering the context of Song of Solomon. Let's look at verses 4-6:

> Song of Solomon 2:4-6, ""He has brought me to his banquet hall, and his banner over me is love. 5 "Sustain me with raisin cakes, refresh me with apples, because I am lovesick. 6 "Let his left hand be under my head and his right hand embrace me."

The reference to "his banner" is a reference to "desire" so that there is a longing for sexual intimacy. In verse 5 "raisin cakes" were to enhance sexual desire. Again, in verse 5 she describes her affection as "lovesick" because she is exhausted from her love for Solomon.

Which means this passage isn't describing two people who are prudish and shy. Instead, this is two people standing before each other who are sexually interested but waiting for the commitment of marriage. Look at verse 7:

> Song of Solomon 2:7, "7 "I adjure you, O daughters of Jerusalem, by the gazelles or by the hinds of the field, **that you do not arouse or awaken my love until she pleases**."

This language "do not arouse or awaken love until she pleases" is incredibly helpful. The gazelle and the deer are both skittish animals, and a sexual relationship is explosive, but you don't want to casually rush into a sexual relationship.

You want the beauty of sex to take place in the commitment of marriage, and the biblical foundation of marriage is established in Genesis 2.

Our psychologists may call it "oxytocin" and "sex glue" but Genesis 2 calls it becoming "one flesh" in marriage because you want the multi-layered parts of a sexual relationship to take place in the divine commitment of marriage. [23]

Our culture says, "Oh, you can be casual about it." You can bounce in and out. You can live together. You can test it out and see if it works. You have to make sure you're sexually compatible!

Are you kidding? What do you think happens when you put two people together who are full of insecurities, fear, anxiety, get them naked, expose their greatest vulnerabilities, release all these chemicals in their brain, and then say, "let's see what happens?"

No, you want the Genesis 2 biblical foundation of marriage so that when you release the supernatural sexual explosion of Song of Solomon 2, it is an explosion that is taking place in the commitment of marriage.

---

[23] Douglas Hofstadter, "I Am A Strange Loop."

For example, when you see the fires in California, those fires are out of control. There are winds blowing from every direction, there are dry conditions in the land, there is an absence of manpower to control the fires, and as a result the damage from a fire is filled with grief.

But, if you take that same powerful force of a fire, and you place that fire in the safety of a fireplace, then everyone hovers around the fireplace for goodness and warmth.

It is similar with sex in marriage because it is in the glory of marriage that we see a husband and wife make a commitment to one another that is strong enough to cradle the powerful gift of sex.

If you're reading this chapter and you are thinking, "Yeah, but I have made some really horrible decisions with sex." You need to know that Jesus came for the horrible decisions.

Jesus has come to draw out our stories of shame and darkness and shine His glorious light into those dark places of our lives. Jesus hasn't come for the purpose of condemnation, but for the purpose of confession, repentance, forgiveness and restoration.

The cleansing Jesus has to offer is because Jesus takes all our pain upon Himself at the cross, putting it to death, so that through His resurrection we might be cleansed and made new.

It doesn't mean those memories of confusion and pain go away, or even disappear, but it does mean they are disarmed, cleansed, and through Jesus we can find new pleasures, new passion, and a new vision to create new memories.

Is it possible that we might drift back to those old pleasures and old passions? Yes, but Jesus is faithful. In those moments Jesus doesn't flinch.

No, in those moments Jesus calls out to us, "That's not who you are any longer. Those things have been put to death. You have been made new. Trust Me, walk in Me. Might all of us respond by turning to Jesus! Consider 1 Corinthians 6:

> 1 Corinthians 6:19-20, "19 Or do you not know that your body is a temple of the Holy Spirit within you, whom you have from God, and that you are not your own? 20 For you have been bought for a price: therefore glorify God in your body."

Reflective Questions:
1. How have your personal experiences shaped this conversation today?
2. Why is our body, and what we do with our body, important to the God of Scripture?

Additional Resources:
- The Four Loves by C.S. Lewis.
- Lost by Christian Smith.
- Benefits of Delaying Sex Until Marriage by Bill Hendrick.
- Is Pornography Addictive by Kirsten Weir.

What About Racism?

Discussing racism is incredibly difficult. By God's grace, North Village Church has experienced some ethnic diversity, and we pray that trend continues. But because we have some ethnic diversity means we are not all coming to this conversation with the same experiences in life.

As a result, when we enter into this conversation with one another it is going to be easy to misunderstand one another.

Therefore, as we begin this chapter, we encourage everyone to lead out with humility and patience because this conversation can be very difficult.

In this chapter we will focus on three sub-points:

1. Define The Conversation.
2. How Does God's Word Respond?
3. How Do We Respond Practically?

1. Define The Conversation.

Like many of our conversations it is easy to get lost in communication, so let's frame our conversation with a definition to help us all stay on the same page.

> Definition: Racism is when we violate (thought, word, and deed) the divine truth (Genesis 1:26-27) that all humans have equal dignity and worth.

There are many ways this can take place in our lives today, but probably the conversation that is taking place most often in our culture today is the tension between white people (majority culture) and people of color (minority culture.)

This phrase "majority culture" might be a new term for some of us, but the reality is that every context we walk into every day has a majority culture influence, and if we aren't aware of the "majority culture" influence it is because we are the "majority culture" influence. [24]

Now the good news is this isn't just a challenge for people based on the color of our skin. We are all constantly navigating majority and minority culture in a variety of areas of our lives, depending on the context we find ourselves.

We might be a man in a room full of women. We might be a little overweight in a room full of six-pack abs. We might be unfamiliar with comic books at a comic book convention,

---

[24] Jerome Gay, "Dominent and Subdominate Cultrual Dynamics", *The Gospel Coalition.* November 12, 2020. https://www.thegospelcoalition.org/podcasts/as-in-heaven/dominant-and-subdominant-cultural-dynamics/

and as a result, there are many opportunities for us in humanity to "violate (thought, word, and deed) the divine truth (Genesis 1:26-27) that all humans have equal dignity and worth."

There are many ways we could explore this conversation, but for the sake of simplicity we are going to draw out the tension between black people and white people, and the black person's experience in the United States historically. Consider the following timeline for black Americans in the United States:

Trans-Atlantic Slave Trade (1525-1860) – 12.5 million Africans are shipped to North America against their will, so that an entire group of people are launched into our nation's history.

Emancipation Proclamation (1863) – In the 1700's the Abolitionist movement is established, largely influenced by Genesis 1, that all humans have dignity and worth. But in 1863 we need to imagine what life would have been like for the black person's newfound freedom. A black person's life would still have been incredibly difficult. A black person would have had very little education, no net-worth, no social network. Their life would have been completely turned upside down.

First Generation (1888) – There was a brief period, known as the Reconstruction Era, where we see our first black lawyers, doctors and educators, but that ends in 1877. And we are guessing the primary focus of a black person would have been survival.

Second Generation (1913) – As a black American your grandfather was a slave, and we are guessing that thought never left their mind.

In addition, the Jim Crow laws of the south are in full effect. If you haven't read about the Jim Crow laws, you should. The oppression at this time is so bad that we see the Great Migration where 6 million black people migrate from the south to northern parts of our country. [25]

Again, one must assume, at this point, that the average black person recovering from slavery has very little education, very little net-worth, very little social network. So basic skills in life like health care, parenting, marriage, and budgeting are at a bare minimum.

Third Generation (1938) – Jim Crow laws are in full effect. An average black person might be getting some education, but again one must assume that it is incredibly challenging to create stability.

Perhaps there is a part of us that is thinking, "But that was in the past, "Why does it matter?" We're not trying to feel sorry for people, but it would be naïve to say to ourselves, "Their story is just like my story."

We're trying to understand the unique challenges that are in our history and seeing the broad scope can help us understand the tension of our conversation today.

Fourth Generation (1963) – We are on the verge of the Civil Rights Movement. Jim Crow laws are about to be dismantled in legislation, but we know

---

[25] David French, "Loving Your Country Means Teaching Its History Honestly," *Time*, July 2, 2021, https://time.com/6077605/american-history-patriotism/

human beings don't change over night. So good things are happening, but it is still likely incredibly difficult for a black person to get a good education, grow net-worth, and a strong social network.

Fifth Generation (1988) – A black person would have had access to some education, some net-worth, and some social network, but it doesn't take a strong imagination to assume that there are going to still be challenges at the parenting level and marital level.

Sixth Generation (2013) – Current generation.

What does this timeline mean? So many times today we assume if a person has problems in life it is because a person made decisions that created those problems.

There are some truths to that statement, but it is overly simplifying the greater complexities of life. And as followers of Jesus, we would do well to try to understand everyone's story and background because everyone has dignity and value in life, and the better we understand one another the more likely we are to be able to live out the truths of Genesis 1.

2. How Does God's Word Respond?

Let's talk about God's Word. How does a follower of Jesus respond to this conversation? Before we read God's Word, we want to acknowledge how easy it is for our hearts to push back on this conversation.

None of us want to see ourselves as racist. We all like the idea of pointing the finger at how others are racist. But in God's Word we see racism isn't a modern-day problem. Racism isn't a United States problem. Racism isn't a white person problem, and racism isn't a slavery problem, but a humanity problem. Let's look at Genesis 1:26-27:

> Genesis 1:26-27, "26 Then God said, "Let Us make man in **Our image**, according to **Our likeness**; and let them rule over the fish of the sea and over the birds of the sky and over the cattle and over all the earth, and over every creeping thing that creeps on the earth." 27 God created man in **His own image**, in the image of God He created him; male and female He created them.""

In Genesis 1 we see clearly that all of humanity is valuable because all of humanity is made in the image of God. Our culture says humanity is valuable if we are attractive, popular, wealthy, compassionate or caring, and we see those values changing every day based on the trends of the day.

But God's Word teaches us, in chapter 1, that our value in humanity is because we are made in His image. Being made in "His image" means humanity carries royal and relational implications as we share in God's stewardship over creation.

Did you catch that? Genesis 1 teaches us humanity carries royal and relational implications because we are made in His image, so that in Genesis 1 we see it isn't just kings and priests who are crowned with this glory and honor, but all of humanity is crowned with glory and honor because we are all made in His image.

That's why we care about how people are treated at the border, how many children are in orphanages, how many children are aborted, because all human life is valuable. This is God's design from the beginning!

—

56

But we know Genesis 3 is coming. [26] We know sin is going to distort all that was created to be good. We know the sin of humanity has rippled into creation (Romans 8:22-23).

As early as Exodus 1:8-14 we see racism enter the story of humanity as God's chosen people (Israel) experience enslavement and oppression. So, the idea of one group of people overpowering another group of people is not just in our nation's history, but a pattern throughout human history.

Sometimes in our culture you will hear people make the observation "Is racism just a few bad apples, or is the whole tree of humanity filled with racism?" Have you heard this phrase?

Genesis 3 makes it clear racism is not "just a few bad apples." Racism is absolutely layered throughout the whole tree of humanity. But are we under the impression the humanity can create a structure without racism?

Are we under the impression that people of color are without flaws? Are we under the impression that women will lead humanity without flaws? Are we under the impression that colonialism is the reason we see brokenness in our world today?

It is because of our sin in Genesis 3 that we can be sure that no matter what institution we construct in humanity we will see brokenness, racism and oppression as one

---

[26] Genesis 3:6-8, "⁶ When the woman saw that the tree was good for food, and that it was a delight to the eyes, and that the tree was desirable to make *one* wise, she took some of its fruit and ate; and she also gave *some* to her husband with her, and he ate. ⁷ Then the eyes of both of them were opened, and they knew that they were naked; and they sewed fig leaves together and made themselves waist coverings."

group of people overpowers another group of people, because this is a pattern throughout humanity. It doesn't mean this pattern of brokenness is okay, but we need to be clear on how easy racism slips into humanity.

3. How Do We Respond Practically?

We pray. There is power in prayer. We want to pray that our hearts would be softened to how racism might show up in our lives toward others.

We empathize. Bearing one another's burdens is to understand the pain of one another; therefore, we want to listen to other people's experiences. Especially if you are the majority culture in any setting. The more we can become aware of other's experiences the stronger our relationships will be with one another.

We want to share our stories with one another. Yes, it's slow to share our stories with one another, but it is great to hear from one another about our experiences.

When there is civil unrest and protests in the street, many white people turn to their Black friends. They ask, "Why is this happening?" "Why is everyone so angry?" "Will you tell me your experience?" In other words, "Will you educate me and tell me what I missed?"

Those are good questions to ask a friend. But it's important for us to invest some time and energy educating ourselves instead of solely relying on others. Perhaps, we should pick up a good book to learn about not only the nation's history but also the church's history.

We want to submit our experiences to God's Word. Our personal stories are powerful, but there's nothing that has happened in our lives outside of His will. Therefore, we can submit our greatest pains to Him and trust Him.

We can't freak out when people don't agree. We are going to disagree on certain things and there is going to be an impulse to shut down, cut off, push away, and post something on social media.

But instead, let us focus on where we agree and celebrate those things. We can all rally around growing in God's Word, the cross of Christ, the love for people, and the 100's of areas where we do have agreement.

We want to stay in the conversation. When we talk about racism it is easy to feel isolated, different and misunderstood. But the answer can't be to seek out people who look like us and think like us and tell ourselves, "I am seeking out diversity."

What about groups like Black Lives Matter? God's Word absolutely teaches us that black lives matter, so that isn't a debate. And, at the same time, there are values in the organization of Black Lives Matter that don't align with God's Word. As a church family we're not going to align with organization that don't align with God's Word.

What about Critical Race Theory? Perhaps some of us have never heard that term, but it is in the news more and more these days. So, we do want to respond quickly.

Critical Race Theory is often characterized as either the hope for humanity, or the downfall of our country, and it's both. There are things in Critical Race Theory that can help us empathize with others, and there are things in Critical Race

Theory that are contrary to God's Word. Now, more than ever, we need to be on the alert, leaning in and filtering the ideas of our day through God's Word.

We want to be agents of reconciliation. The God of Scripture is for justice. Therefore, we want to look for ways to reflect His heart in this world. We can volunteer, we can vote, we can run for office, foster children, mentor / tutor, care for the elderly, but do something to cross racial barriers to extend His heart toward others.

We need to seek out opportunities of diversity. We can't settle for our own little circle of familiarity. We must seek out relationships with people who are different than us. In the end, we wish we could tell you that at North Village Church you will never feel misunderstood, never feel out of place, never feel marginalized, but we know that's not true.

We know we are going to hurt one another, and the gospel is that Jesus has come to take all of our hurts upon Himself at the cross and conquer them in the resurrection, so that by grace through faith in Jesus we are called His.

This is the beauty of the local church. Our culture is looking for justice, hope, transformation, and there's no greater answers for the hurts in our world than the life we know in Jesus. [27]

Reflective Questions:
1. How do you see racism or bias based on ethnicity showing up in your relationships today?

---

[27]David Brooks, "The Strage Persistance of Guilt,"New York Times, March 31, 2017.https://www.nytimes.com/2017/03/31/opinion/the-strange-persistence-of-guilt.html

2. What are the tangible steps you can take today to learn about different perspectives others have experienced?

Additional Resources:
- Is CRT Marxist? Consider reading a short article called, "Reflections from a Christian scholar on Social Justice, Critical Race Theory, Marxism, and Biblical Ethics" by Kelly Hamren.
- Reading While Black by Esau McCaulley.
- The Color of Compromise by Jamar Tisby.
- One Blood: Parting Words to the Church on Race by John M. Perkins.
- The Cross and the Lynching Tree by James Cone.

What About American Christianity?

Research shows that most Democratic and Republican voters live in partisan bubbles with little exposure to those who belong to the other party.

A study done March 16, 2021, found that most Democrats and Republicans live in levels of segregation that exceed racial segregation in our past. [28]

I am sure there are many local churches where that stat would prove to be true, but the Lord has blessed North Village Church with political diversity. You might not know it, but you are likely sitting next to someone on a

---

[28] Christina Pazzanese, "Democrats and Republicans do live in different worlds," The Harvard Gazette, March 16, 2021, https://news.harvard.edu/gazette/story/2021/03/democrats-and-republicans-live-in-partisan-bubbles-study-finds/

Sunday morning who votes completely different, and that's why this conversation is important for our church family.

In this chapter we will focus on three sub-points:

1. Define The Conversation.
2. How Does God's Word Respond?
3. How Do We Respond Practically?

1. Define the Conversation.

In Matthew 7 Jesus is teaching to the crowds and asks the question, "Why do you look at the speck that in your brother's eye, but do not notice the log that is in your own eye?"

It is likely that we see this question being applied to the political discourse of our day as Republicans and Democrats seem to spot the weaknesses and flaws in the other party but struggle to see the giant problems that exist in their own party. And again, this oversight makes this conversation very complicated. [29]

Probably the most common critique on both sides is that "These people need to stop tarnishing the good name of Jesus!"

If you lean Democratic you are confident that the Republican Party is taking Bible verses, the name of Jesus, "God's chosen nation"- type of language and weaving it into their political agendas and giving Jesus a bad name.

---

[29] Leo Tolstoy, "Three Methods of Reform" in Pamphlets: Translated from the Russian (1900).

And, if you lean Republican, you are confident that the Democratic Party is taking bible verses, name of Jesus, "Hands and feet of Jesus" - type of language and weaving it into their political agendas and giving Jesus a bad name.

But we would do well to remember both political parties are layering their agendas with biblical themes because both Democratic and Republican parties have values that come out of the Scriptures. [30]

Generally speaking, Democrats are going to lean toward biblical values like mercy, grace and compassion. And Republicans are going to lean toward truth, law, right and wrong, which are also biblical. Therefore, when we enter into this conversation, we want to be careful that we aren't pitting biblical values against biblical values. [31]

Generally speaking, if a person votes Democratic it is often because that person believes the challenges and hardships in our nation are because of broken systems and structures. Therefore, it is the responsibility of the government to repair those broken systems and structures. But, then what does that person do with Proverbs 10:4:

> Proverbs 10:4, "Lazy hands make for poverty, but diligent hands bring wealth."

What does a follower of Jesus do with this verse? This verse looks like the reason for challenges and hardships

---

[30] Charles A. Colson, "What's Right About the Religious Right," Christianity Today, September 6, 1999,
https://www.christianitytoday.com/ct/1999/september6/9ta058.html

[31] Jonathan Haidt, The Righteous Mind: Why Good People are Divided By Politics and Religion. (New York: Vintage Books, 2012), 109.

in our nation are not systemic but based on individual character and choices.

Again, generally speaking, a person who votes Republican is often times motivated by an individual taking personal responsibility. A Republican voter probably loves Proverbs 10:4. But what does a Republican voter do with Proverbs 13:23?

> Proverbs 13:23, "An unplowed field produces food for the poor, but injustice sweeps it away."

What does a follower of Jesus do with this verse? The word "injustice" isn't individual injustice, but a reference to the non-religious legal systems of the land.

The person who votes Democratic is probably jumping up and down, posting this verse on social media, because when sinners make up a nation and create systems you are going to see systemic problems.

Therefore, what do we do with these two tensions in scripture? How do we not pit biblical principles against one another for the sake of politics? Are we going to point the finger at the other party, and only see their offenses? Are we going to assume everyone else is an idiot and only our political goals are honoring to Jesus?

God's Word teaches us that the hope of the local church isn't getting everyone to be only Republican or only Democrat, but the hope of the local church is the body of Christ coming under the Lordship of Jesus in such a way that we work together and honor Him!

Imagine a local church where biblical values of the Democratic Party and Republican Party are both honored and esteemed. Imagine a local church where mercy, grace, truth and law are both elevated and pursued. This is our dream at North Village Church.

Now, it's possible you are thinking, "Yeah, but I know some Democrats and some Republicans who have taken those biblical values, and absolutely applied those biblical values in an unbiblical way." That's true!

We can take "mercy" too far. Sometimes the Democratic Party is so bent on mercy that the Democratic Party will justify violence to enforce mercy! See the riots of 2020. That's not good.

And we can take "truth and law" too far. Sometimes the Republican Party will justify excessive force because rules weren't followed. See how people are being treated at the border in 2020-2021.

That's why now, more than ever, we need one another. We don't need to villainize one another, cut one another off, and dismiss one another. Instead, we need the Spirit of God to help us to see how we are better together, and together we might see the beauty of Jesus lived out in His people. It can happen!

2. How Does God's Word Respond?

We could look at Mark 12, "Give to Caesar that which is Caesar's." We could look at Romans 13, "be subject to governing authorities."

Or we could look at Philippians 3 as the Apostle Paul refers to followers of Jesus as "heavenly citizens." But we want us to see how Jesus engages the political tensions of the day when Jesus is tempted by Satan.

Matthew 4:1, "1 Then Jesus was led up by the Spirit into the wilderness to be tempted by the devil."

Perhaps you know this passage, or perhaps you are reading it for the first time. But in Matthew 4, Jesus has been presented as God in the flesh (Matthew 3), and like Adam and Eve of old, we see the devil trying to distract Jesus from His ultimate purpose. Look at verses 2-4:

Matthew 4:2-4, "2 And after He had fasted for forty days and forty nights, He then became hungry. 3 And the tempter came and said to Him, "If You are the Son of God, command that these stones become bread." 4 But He answered and said, "It is written: 'Man shall not live on bread alone, but on every word that comes out of the mouth of God.'"

In verses 2-4 we see Jesus has been fasting for 40 days, Jesus is hungry, and in a moment of hunger the enemy comes with an offering of something as simple as food.

Did you need to know we have an enemy who is going to prey upon us when we are tired, hungry and beaten down by life. 1 Peter 5:8 teaches us the devil prowls around like a roaring lion seeking someone to devour, and the devil's ultimate purpose is to distract us from our ultimate calling and purpose in life.

You might be saying to yourself right now, "Are you talking about demonic and satanic influences?" Yes. There are forces of darkness that are absolutely working against any progress of His Kingdom, any acts of kindness, and any relationships of unity that we might try to pursue today.

Please don't think the evils of humanity today are just because of social media influences and political agendas are creating division.

Please don't think the examples of abortion and racism we see today are just about women's rights and equality, because every act of division we see in our day is being influenced by the evil one.

Even on a personal level, we would do well to acknowledge every thought we have doesn't originate in our own heart and mind, but we have an enemy who wants to kill, steal and destroy (John 10:10). Look at verses 5-7:

> Matthew 4:5-7, "5 Then the devil took Him along into the holy city and had Him stand on the pinnacle of the temple, 6 and he said to Him, "If You are the Son of God, throw Yourself down; for it is written: 'He will give His angels orders concerning You'; and 'On their hands they will lift You up, so that You do not strike Your foot against a stone.' 7 Jesus said to him, "On the other hand, it is written: 'You shall not put the Lord your God to the test.'"

In verses 5-7 Satan is tempting Jesus to trust in Himself. Satan is tempting Jesus to doubt the Father's provision and protection with accusations like, "If you are the Son of God."

In that moment Satan is tempting Jesus to get swept up in fear of what might happen if Jesus doesn't take His life into His own hands. In that moment Satan is tempting Jesus to doubt the Father's provision and protection in His life.

In the same way, we would do well to be on guard to temptation when we find ourselves in political discussions. Are we being tempted to become swept up in fear of what might happen? Are we being tempted to doubt the Father's provision and protection? Are we being tempted to believe, "God doesn't care. God isn't doing anything. I need to make something happen."

Is it possible we might find ourselves so engulfed in a political conversation that we say to ourselves, "I don't care what Scripture says, I have to do what I have to do?" In those moments we need to remember there are forces of darkness at work in this world, and we need to be on guard. Look at verses 8-11:

> Matthew 4:8-11, "8 Again, the devil took Him along to a very high mountain and showed Him all the kingdoms of the world and their glory; 9 and he said to Him, "All these things I will give You, if You fall down and worship me." 10 Then Jesus said to him, "Go away, Satan! For it is written: 'You shall worship the Lord your God, and serve Him only.'" 11 Then the devil left Him; and behold, angels came and began to serve Him.

There are several things we could pull out of Matthew 4, but for the sake of simplicity, let's focus on Jesus being tempted with the glory of this world (Verse 8).

In verse 8 Jesus is tempted with the glory of this world, and yet Jesus' eyes were always on the Father and His Kingdom. This is what is most important in our lives as followers of Jesus.

There are areas where our allegiance to Jesus coincides with leaders, politics and earthly governments, and those moments are great, but at any divergence we always need to side with Jesus.

This is easier to write on a page than to live out in life, but this is our challenge for today. We must always sift the news of the day through God's Word. We must be diligent to examine our heart and motives. We must be building relationships with men and women who will speak into our lives when we are drifting from the Lord because the temptation is great.

3. How Do We Respond Practically?

At North Village Church there are some guiding principles that have served us well, and below are a few principles we have found to be helpful in this conversation.

1. We create a welcoming environment for all political views. Did you know Jesus calls two different types of political perspectives to be His disciples?

Matthew the Tax Collector (Matthew 9) and Simon the Zealot (Luke 6) both come from different political perspectives, and both are called to follow Jesus.

As a tax collector, Matthew would have collaborated with the Roman occupiers, who were extorting the people of Israel, and Matthew, an Israelite, would have helped the Roman government oppress his own people.

Simon the Zealot would have had a completely different relationship with the Roman government. A Zealot is basically connected to a terrorist organization that made raids and revolts against Roman occupation, and yet Jesus calls both Matthew and Simon into the same group of disciples. Isn't that interesting?

Surely when Simon the Zealot responds to Jesus he leaves behind his anger, temper and rage for the Roman Empire. And surely when Matthew, the Tax Collector, responds to Jesus he leaves behind his business, networks and relationships with the Roman Empire. But don't you think they didn't leave those things behind 100%?

Surely, they still had their bents for or against the Roman Empire on some level. Surely, they still had their personalities, their leanings, their interests, and yet we see in God's good wisdom He brings both of these types of people together as disciples.

It would have been easier to just bring one or none, but Jesus brings both. Therefore, might we create a welcoming environment for political interests as we all submit our lives to Jesus as Lord.

Might we extend grace toward one another? Might we be gentle with our words toward one another? Might we convey a posture of humility as we learn from one another, because in the life of Jesus we see Matthew and Simon finding a welcome home with Him.

2. Is America The New Israel or The New Babylon? This might be confusing, but there are two broad eras in Israel's history.

The first is their history as a nation and the second is Israel's history in captivity. Therefore, as followers of Jesus today, it is common to see some who are trying to build a Christian nation, like Israel of old, and there are some who believe we are to live as exiles in a strange land. [32]

Augustine tells us the answer is both. Government is ordained by God. Therefore, as followers of Jesus, we are called to be involved. [33]

We are called to seek justice. We are called to be a blessing. We are called to influence. We are called to be the best citizens we can be, and at the same time government is not the only calling we have in Christ.

We can't give ourselves fully to our nation's citizenship because we are also called to our heavenly citizenship (Philippians 3:20) as brothers and sisters in Christ, husbands and wives, fathers and mothers in the body of Christ.

3. Might we hold tight to the gospel. It's possible the world around us will look at our faith in Jesus' life, death and resurrection and says, "Who could possibly believe in something so fantastic?" Something so outdated? Surely, we need to evolve as a people.

But every human being is placing his or her trust and confidence in something in life. In every one of these cultural conversations in this booklet we are holding a

---

[32] James Davidson Hunter, Culture Wars: The Struggle to Define America. (New York: Basicbooks, 1991), 161-2.

[33] St. Augustine, The City of God, Chapter 28: Of the Nature of the Two Cities, the Earthly and the Heavenly, section 283.

position and response, and every position and response begin with an authority, and at the end of the day we are all trusting that authority is reliable.

It might be another faith system in the world that shapes our views, or it might be our own experience and education that shapes our views, or it might be a hodge-podge of beliefs that shapes our views, but as a human being we are all putting our trust in something.

As followers of Jesus, we are trusting the man in Matthew 4 is God in the flesh. As a follower of Jesus, we are trusting the suffering servant who defeats the temptations of this world. As followers of Jesus we are trusting in the One who takes the brokenness of our world upon Himself at the cross and conquers our brokenness in the resurrection, so that as followers of Jesus the Kingdom of Heaven is now!

We don't just believe Jesus is true because of warm fuzzies, family background or tradition. We believe Jesus is true because of concrete, historical evidence in the lives of men and women who saw Jesus, heard Jesus, touched Jesus, and gave their lives to Jesus (New Testament).

This is the credible authority we put our trust in, and every person in humanity has to look at the authority figures in life and ask themselves, "Have those authorities lived under the scrutiny of time like Jesus? Have those authorities given their life for the sake of those positions? Are those authorities' transforming lives and bearing fruit of peace, joy, patience and kindness toward others?"

Even greater, will those authorities of our day be able to gather a people from all over the globe, every walk of life, to be a people who voluntarily lay aside their preferences to become a new people?

There's nobody or nothing like Jesus! If you've never believed in Jesus, you need to today.

Reflective Questions:
1. How would you know if you are holding on to political positions too tightly?
2. When is the last time you had a conversation with someone who had different political views?

Additional Resources:
- Dietrich Bonhoeffer, "Ethics."
- Timothy Keller, "How Do Christians Fit Into the Two Party System? They Don't."
- Is the Church Too Woke? A Letter From N.T. Wright.

What About Homosexuality?

This conversation is really complicated and uncomfortable. It's complicated because we all have unique sexual desires. There is nobody that has 100% the same sexual desires as someone else.

What one person finds desirable, another person might find objectionable, and visa-versa, because our sexual desires are different.

We feel different things, we are attracted to different people, and that makes it impossible to capture this conversation completely in a few pages.

In addition, this conversation is uncomfortable. Historically followers of Jesus haven't done a great job of engaging any conversation around sexuality, and as a result there is multiple layers of baggage when we engage this conversation with others.

Therefore, as we enter into this conversation, our hope isn't to push a particular view, but more so frame the conversation for us and then invite us to wrestle with God's Word as we engage this conversation together.

In this chapter we will focus on three sub-points:

1. Is It Possible?
2. How Does God's Word Respond?
3. What Are The Objections?

1. Is It Possible?

There are many directions we could explore on homosexuality, but at the heart of many of our conversations today is the question, "Is it possible to have homosexual desires and still call yourself a follower of Jesus?"

Before we can start to engage this question, we want to begin with some basic definitions to help us all stay on the same page.

> **Follower of Jesus:** A follower of Jesus is someone who sees Jesus as Lord over every area of our lives, someone who has decided to turn from sin, to trust and obey Jesus by grace through faith.

It is important to clarify that we are not using the word "Christian" intentionally. Someone might call themselves a "Christian" if they are American, attend Baylor

University, grew up in a Christian home, or even attend a local church, but we are using the phrase "follower of Jesus" because when we ask this question we are talking about someone who is a disciple of Jesus.

In addition, when we say "homosexuality" we are talking about this specific definition.

> **Homosexuality:** When a person is attracted to a person of the same sex. Importantly, the physical act of two same sex people having sex is the expression of homosexuality, not necessarily the sum total of the person.

This distinction is important as we get into the conversation. Many times, when we hear the word "homosexuality," we tend to zero in on the sexual behavior of homosexual desires instead of the description of a desire that a person has toward the same sex.

Did you catch the difference? Our culture today teaches us that homosexuality is an identity, but how could someone's sexual desires possibly make up the totality of one's identity? [34]

We wouldn't make that same conclusion with heterosexual desires. We wouldn't say a heterosexual person's identity is their heterosexuality. And we wouldn't want to conclude that all people with homosexual desires have the same identity because they have homosexual desires.

---

[34] Is Homosexuality An Identity? https://pubmed.ncbi.nlm.nih.gov/6376621/

Instead, homosexual desires are just that, homosexual desires. Genesis 1 and 2 make it clear that all of humanity was created to be perfect, and all of humanity was created with perfect sexual desires, but because of our sin (Genesis 3) all of humanity and our sexual desires have been damaged and broken.

We can't stress brokenness of our sin in Genesis 3 enough. All of humanity is created to be aligned with the God of Scripture, but in our sin, there is a fracturing that takes place in our spiritual desires, social desires, and our sexual desires, and that applies to all people.

It's possible that someone might push back and say, "Really, we're going to rely on God's Word to speak into practical areas of our sexual life today?"

But we see these layers of brokenness in every area of our life. We see brokenness in our spiritual desires as we worship things like career, power, status, money, relationships, etc.

We see brokenness in our social desires as we struggle to navigate relationships with one another. We hurt one another, we offend one another, and sometimes we hurt and offend one another when we aren't even trying to hurt and offend one another.

And we see brokenness in our sexual desires through things like promiscuity, polygamy, pornography and homosexuality.

Therefore, when we pose the question, "Is it possible to have homosexual desires and still call yourself a follower of

Jesus?" We must remember that Jesus has come to expose the brokenness of our world (spiritually, socially and sexually) and Jesus invites all people to turn to Him and find life in Him.

One person said it this way, "The invitation of Jesus to the person with homosexual desires is not to have heterosexual desires. The invitation of Jesus is to be holy, and that is an invitation that is given to all people!"[35]

Therefore, the answer to the question is, "Yes." A follower of Jesus can have homosexual desires, but those homosexual desires are not their ultimate because Jesus has come to give us new desires in Him.

2. How Does God's Word Respond To Homosexuality?

Let's look at 1 Corinthians 6. The Corinthian church is absolutely in the middle of a culture that was indifferent towards Jesus.

If you read this letter on your own you will see a people with broken spiritual, social and sexual desires, and you will see people who are learning to submit those spiritual, social and sexual desires to Jesus.

You will see people getting drunk at communion (1 Corinthians 11), abstaining from sex in marriage (1 Corinthians 7), having sex with their mother-in-law (1 Corinthians 5), and in verses 1-8 we see the Apostle Paul admonishing the Corinthian church to stop taking one another to court. Let's look at verses 7-8:

---

[35] Jackie Hill Perry, "The Heterosexual Gospel."
https://www.desiringgod.org/articles/the-heterosexual-gospel

1 Corinthians 6:7-8, "7 Actually, then, it is already a defeat for you, that you have lawsuits with one another. Why not rather suffer the wrong? Why not rather be defrauded? 8 On the contrary, you yourselves do wrong and defraud. And this to your brothers and sisters!"

This might seem out of place for the content of this chapter, but it's important to see the pattern of God's Word speaking into every area of our lives, not just our sexual desires.

It is because of our sin (Genesis 3) we are spiritually broken, socially broken, sexually broken, and Jesus has come to invite us to find life in Him. Unfortunately, the good news of Jesus is difficult for us to see today and it's likely difficult to see because we have lived for so long in our brokenness.

A number of years ago there was a cruise ship that got stuck off the coast of Italy and eventually turned on its side while passengers were still aboard. In order for the passengers to exit they had to walk out of the ship sideways! [36]

[36] Inside the Wreck of the Costa Concordia, The Atlantic. January 20, 2012. https://www.theatlantic.com/photo/2012/01/inside-the-wreck-of-the-costa-concordia/100229/

The passengers had to walk on walls, climb through windows and step over doors, but the passengers said, "In the beginning it was awkward, but eventually it felt normal to go through the ship sideways."

That's a little bit of what life is like after Genesis 3. We have lived so long in a world of hurt, pain, and brokenness that we think hurt, pain and brokenness is normal.

But the good news of Jesus is that Jesus has come to put back into place that which He intended from the very beginning. Jesus has come to heal our broken spiritual, social and sexual desires so that we can find life as He intended, in Him. Let's look at verses 9-10:

> 1 Corinthians 6:9-10, "9 Or do you not know that the **unrighteous will not inherit the kingdom of God**? Do not be deceived; neither the sexually immoral, nor idolaters, nor adulterers, nor homosexuals, 10 nor thieves, nor the greedy, nor those habitually drunk, nor verbal abusers, nor swindlers, will inherit the kingdom of God.

We're not sure why, but for some reason people tend to focus on the word "homosexual" in verse 9. But again, the list is to highlight our spiritual brokenness (idolatry), sexual brokenness (adultery), and social brokenness (greed).

Therefore, it's important to place our focus on the phrase "the unrighteous will not inherit the kingdom of God" because that doesn't apply to some people but all people because all people are sinners.

Romans 3 teaches us, "None of us are righteous, none of us understand the glory of God, none of us seek God," and the gospel is Jesus has come to invite all people to see our brokenness and turn to Him and find life in Him.

3. What Are The Objections?

A. Jesus never spoke out against homosexuality?
While it's true Jesus is never recorded saying the word "homosexuality." But it's not true that Jesus never spoke to our sexuality.

In Mark 10 we see Jesus reference Genesis 1, and in Genesis 1-2 we see Adam was with God, and yet described as being "alone" so that the solution wasn't an animal to bring to Adam, it wasn't another man to bring to Adam, but it was a woman created from the man to become one flesh in marriage. So, when Jesus references Genesis 1 Jesus is speaking to our sexuality.

B. What about the Old Testament laws we don't follow?

It is common for people to say, "Why don't we follow some Leviticus laws? Why don't we see followers of Jesus making a big deal about eating pork, shellfish, wearing garments that are woven with two types of material, but just seem to focus on homosexuality?"

Those questions are true, but we need to remember the historical context of those references in the Old Testament. Specifically, those references revolved around the nation of Israel, and when Israel is established as a nation, they are given Civil Laws, Ceremonial Laws and Moral Laws.

When Jesus comes to make us new people in Him, we no longer apply Civil Laws (We're not a nation as followers of Jesus), and we no longer apply Ceremonial Laws (Jesus died

82

and rose), but the Moral Laws (How we treat one another, and how we live) still apply.

C. It was promiscuous homosexuality that was rejected, not committed homosexual relationships.

The argument is that God's Word isn't speaking against homosexuality as long as two people are in a committed, caring relationship.

But we need to be clear that Scripture affirms Genesis 1-2, husband and wife in marriage over and over. So to say, "Well, the bible wasn't ever specific about the types of homosexuality" is like saying, "Well, Scripture says we are made in God's image, but the bible never says we can't trip people" so that's okay.

When Scripture speaks to marriage between a husband and wife in Genesis 2, we can be confident scripture speaks to homosexuality.

D. I was born this way.

There is debate that homosexuality is the result of nature, how we are born, or the result of nurture, how we are influenced. [37] The reality is that homosexual desires are probably a combination of nature and nurture, but for the follower of Jesus, this objection doesn't carry any weight.

All of humanity is born with broken sexual desires, Genesis 3, and by grace through faith in Jesus; we are all invited to turn from how we are born and / or influenced and submitting our lives to Jesus as Lord.

---

[37] Sexual Orientation and Suicidality: A Co-Twin Control Study in Adult Men," in Gagnon.

E. Are homosexuals really welcome at North Village Church?

There are two kinds of people at North Village Church: Attendees and Partners. Those who are attending are investigating our church family but have not officially locked arms with us through partnership. The door is wide open to explore and investigate.

The Partner at North Village Church is a follower of Jesus who is submitting their desires to Jesus as Lord over every area of their lives as they live a life of confession and repentance until we are face to face with Him in eternity. That is a pattern we apply to all Partners.

Let us close with a reminder of why Jesus is so important by looking at 1 Corinthians 6:11 as the Apostle Paul lists all these desires, and then writes:

> 1 Corinthians 6:11, "11 Such were some of you; but you were washed, but you were sanctified, but you were justified in the name of the Lord Jesus Christ and in the Spirit of our God."

The Apostle Paul helps us to see that the church at Corinth was made up of people who had engaged in the lifestyles of adultery, idolatry, homosexuality, greed, drunkenness, and then in verse 11 says, "Such were some of you, but you were washed, sanctified, justified in the name of Jesus."

So that the Corinthian church was made up of men, women, and children who turned from the broken desires of this world and submitted those desires to Jesus as Lord of their lives so that they became ex-adulterers, ex-idolaters, ex-homosexuals. It is because Jesus changes lives!

Hebrews 4 teaches us in Jesus we have someone who can not only sympathize with our weakness, but One who has been tempted in all things as we are, yet without sin.

Pause there for a moment. Take all those desires that we have been thinking and talking about for a minute and consider Jesus is the only One in eternity who can say to you, "I understand that desire and temptation."

Therefore, any sexual desires that we might have that are not of Him are ones that we can turn to Jesus and hear Jesus say to us, "I understand you. I love you. Turn to Me. Find life in Me."

Reflective Questions:
1. How is it possible that we are placing too much emphasis on our sexual desires?
2. What does it look like practically to submit our sexual desires to Jesus?

Additional Resources:
- Homosexuality and the Christian by Mark Yarhouse.
- Women, Slaves, and Homosexuals by Robert Webb.
- Sam Allberry, "Why Does God Care Who I Sleep With?"

What About Same Sex Marriage?

We all know this conversation is layered with politics, emotions, government, history, and all those layers make this conversation complicated. But we hope there are some things that are clear as we go through this booklet.

We hope it is clear that God's Word is absolutely against the oppression of all people, no matter their sexual choices.

We hope it is clear that we approach this conversation, and every conversation, with humility because none of us are going through life in a place of superiority.

We hope it is clear that scripture makes it clear we are all sinners. We have all fallen short of God's glory. We have all manifested sexual desires that are contrary to God's Word. But the hope for humanity is that Jesus has come to expose the brokenness of our world so that we might turn to Him and find life in Him. That's the gospel!

It is within the context of the gospel that we talk about same sex marriage. We won't be able to answer every question in this chapter, but we do want to be clear on these three areas:

1. Define The Conversation.
2. Why Is Marriage Important?
3. What Are The Hurdles?

1. Define the Conversation.

When it comes to the conversation around same-sex marriage, we need to start with history. The question of civil unions (not legal marriage) for same sex couples started in the 1970's, but the legal union of marriage began to get traction in 1993 when a Hawaiian Supreme Court ruled that the states prohibition *might* be unconstitutional. [38]

As a result, the Defense of Marriage Act was signed into law by President Bill Clinton in 1996 which held to the position that marriage was one man and one woman and allowed states to refuse to recognize same-sex marriage granted under the laws of others states.

But in 2015 the U.S. Supreme Court struck down all state bans on same-sex marriage, therefore, legalizing same-sex marriage in all fifty states. [39]

---

[38] In Hawaii, Step Toward Legalized Gay Marriage. New York Times, Jeffrey Schmalz, May 7, 1993. https://www.nytimes.com/1993/05/07/us/in-hawaii-step-toward-legalized-gay-marriage.html

[39] Supreme Court Ruling Makes Same-Sex Marriage A Right. New York Times. June 26, 2015. https://www.nytimes.com/2015/06/27/us/supreme-court-same-sex-marriage.html

Today in the United States, all people, regardless of sex, have the opportunity to participate in marriage, so that today there are three primary responses you will see around this conversation:

First, there are some who look at God's Word and conclude that same-sex marriage should be opposed at all levels. This first group concludes:

- God's Word speaks against homosexuality, therefore why would we embrace this as a nation through the establishment of same-sex marriage?
- God's Word describes marriage as one man and one woman, therefore, there is no such thing as "same-sex marriage."
- In addition, a marriage ceremony involves multiple people like decorators, florists, officiants, locations, photographers and our First Amendment should protect people to exercise their beliefs.

Second, there are some who look at God's Word and conclude that same-sex marriage should be supported at all levels. This second group concludes:

- God's Word values all people, therefore, why should all people not have access and availability to the commitment of marriage?
- Oftentimes the second group will compare same-sex marriage to that of inter-racial marriages of the 1950's, and even if people think it is wrong, shouldn't happen, or are uncomfortable, it is obvious to this second group that it should happen.
- In addition, same-sex marriage honors the value of commitment, fidelity and love, which are biblical values, therefore, why would we not want to encourage these values in other people?

Third, there is a third group who look at God's Word and conclude followers of Jesus can do both:

- Support laws that make same-sex marriage available to all people.
- And want to protect religious liberty for those who are uncomfortable providing or performing in same-sex marriages based on their beliefs.

It is important to clarify; the conversation around religious liberty is important. The separation of church and state is a value that is deeply imbedded in our country.

The separation isn't to guard the state from the church, but the separation is to guard the church (faith of the people) from the state because at no point do, we want the federal government telling any faith groups in our country what to believe and not believe.

2. Why Is Marriage Important?

It's possible that we could go back and forth about which view is right or wrong, but it is important that we understand why the gift of marriage is important, and how the gift of marriage has influenced society as a whole. Let's look at Genesis 2:18:

Genesis 2:18, "18 Then the Lord God said, "It is not good for the man to be alone; I will make him a helper suitable for him."

In Genesis 2 we see the God of Scripture zero in on His prized creation, humanity, and when you see the phrase "It is not good for the man to be alone" you are seeing the gift of marriage beginning to be introduced to humanity. Genesis 2 is the first wedding invitation! It's right there!

This phrase, "It is not good for man to be alone" should jump off the page because up to this point, everything God has done in Genesis 1-2 has been, "Good."

God creates light, "Good." God creates land, "Good." God creates life, "Good." But now, in verse 18, Scripture states, "It is not good." What?

Keep in mind this is before sin (Genesis 3), therefore, we have to ask ourselves, "How could anything NOT be good in Genesis 2?" Adam is in the garden face-to-face with God, but in verse 18 Scripture says, "It is not good for the man to be alone" so that verse 18 is a BIG DEAL.

In addition, the gift of marriage isn't just one phrase. As we read, we are going to see God's Word describe what God intended it to look like for a husband and wife in marriage.

Notice at the end of verse 18 it says, "I will make him a helper suitable for him." This subtle phrase is going to introduce what the role of a wife looks like in marriage.

When we see the words like "Helper" and "Suitable" it could make our eyes start twitching because it is language that sounds oppressive toward women. But we know Genesis 1 says, "Male and female are made in the image of God" so this word "Helper" can't mean women are inferior.

In fact, this word "Helper," in the original language, is a word of power. This word "Helper" has a connotation of military reinforcements like, "Oh, no, get the helper!"

This word "Helper" is the same word used of "God as our helper" in Psalm 54. This is the same word that Jesus assigns to the Holy Spirit as "Our Helper" so that in verse

18 the God of Scripture is looking at Adam and saying, "I am going to send him the helper."

And she's not just any old "helper." She's a "suitable helper." Do you see that word in verse 18? The word "suitable" means she's a complimentary helper.

The God of Scripture could have brought in an animal. He could have brought in another man, but the gift of marriage is set apart to be one man, one woman, so that they might compliment one another. Look at verses 19-20:

> Genesis 2:19-20, "19 And out of the ground the Lord God formed every animal of the field and every bird of the sky, and brought them **to the man to see what he would call them**; and whatever the man called a living creature, that was its name. 20 The man gave names to all the livestock, and to the birds of the sky, and to every animal of the field, but for Adam there was not found a helper suitable for him."

In verse 18 we see the divine role of a wife in marriage, and in verses 19-20 we see the divine role of a husband in marriage as Adam is set apart to be a spiritual leader.

Earlier in verse 15 you see Adam given responsibility to care for the garden. In verse 16 you see God speaking directly to Adam to obey God and enjoy God. In verse 19 we see Adam given the responsibility to name creation, so that in Genesis 2 we see the divine role of a husband in marriage as a spiritual leader in marriage.

Now, this language of "spiritual leader" doesn't mean the husband's the boss. This language doesn't mean the husband's more important than the wife.

This role for the husband doesn't mean the husband gets what he wants. The language of "spiritual leader" means someone needs to be responsible for the spiritual health of the marriage, and the God of Scripture has given that responsibility to the husband.

Let's pause for a moment because it's possible you are thinking, "I thought we were talking about same-sex marriage?" We are, but it's important to clarify that we aren't just talking about being "For" or "Against" same-sex marriage as an independent conversation.

We are talking about the gift of marriage and the role that marriage plays in society. [40] Marriage doesn't exist because the government gives us a license to get married. Marriage doesn't exist because we need parties and events to attend for friends and family. [41]

Marriage is a supernatural gift from God that predates government (Genesis 2), and from the very beginning we see there are divine roles for husbands and wives in marriage. [42] Look at verses 21-22:

> Genesis 2:21-22, "21 So the Lord God caused a deep sleep to fall upon the man, and he slept; then He took one of his ribs and closed up the flesh at that place.

---

[40] Robert R. Reilly, Making Gay Okay: How Rationalizing Homosexual Behavior is Changing Everything. (San Francisco: Ignatius Press, 2014), 69.

[41] Brittany Wong, "This Man Took Engagement Photos with a Burrito—And it was Burrito-ful," The Huffington Post, July 13, 2015, http://www.huffingtonpost.com/entry/this-man-took-engagement-photos-with-a-burrito-and-it-was-burrito-ful_55a4268ae4b0a47ac15d27d1

[42] Wayne Grudem, citing Joseph Daniel Unwin, Sex and Culture (London: Oxford University Press, 1934); Sexual Regulations and Cultural Behavior (London: Oxford University Press, 1935); and Hopousia: Or the Sexual and Economic Foundations of a New Society (London: George Allen and Unwin, 1940).

---

22 The Lord God fashioned into a woman the rib which He had taken from the man, and brought her to the man."

In verse 21 the woman comes from the man's rib. One theologian made the observation it isn't from Adam's feet to be under him, or Adam's head to be over him, but his side to be near his heart. [43]

This image is important for us to see when we think about marriage because marriage isn't intended to be a throw away event that we change here and there throughout history.

In verse 22 the God of Scripture is bringing the gift of a wife to a husband so that together they can begin a family. In time those families will become a clan. In time those clans will become a tribe, and in time those tribes will become a nation. It all starts with marriage! [44]

You might not know it, but this image in verse 22 of a wife being given to the husband is why we have the father walk his daughter down the aisle in a wedding. It is a symbolic act to remind us of Genesis 2 as Eve is presented to Adam in marriage.

This is why people at a wedding stand in reverence as the bride enters into the room. It isn't because the bride is the prettiest bride, the purest bride, or the nicest bride, but she's the reminder of Genesis 2-when marriage is introduced to humanity, and these are foundational pieces of a society. Look at how man responds in verse 23:

---

[43] Matthew Henry, An Exposition of the Old and New Testament Volume 6

[44] Andreas Kostenberger, God, Marriage and Family: Rebuilding the Biblical Foundation. (Wheaton: Crossway, 2004), 117

Genesis 2:23, "23 The man said, "This is now bone of my bones, and flesh of my flesh; She shall be called Woman, because she was taken out of Man.""

In verse 23 we see the type of language, which is that of a poem. In the original language it's a song. It's an outburst of excitement. The woman's not a possession to be received. She's a crown to be treasured. It's the gift of marriage being presented in Genesis 2!

Again, it's important to clarify that our purpose in life isn't to get married. It doesn't matter if you are single, married, have heterosexual desires, or homosexual desires, but that all of us would see that biblical marriage is a gift that absolutely ripples into society in ways we could never imagine. Look at verses 24-25:

Genesis 2:24-25, "24 For this reason a man shall leave his father and his mother, and be joined to his wife; and they shall become **one flesh**. 25 And the man and his wife were both naked and were not ashamed."

In verse 24 you see sexual union taking place between husband and wife. We discussed the importance of "one flesh" in our chapter on "Sex Before Marriage" and it's important to highlight again.

The spiritual bond in marriage isn't just ceremonial. There are chemical and biological attachments as man and woman become husband and wife in marriage, so that marriage is a gift to the stability of humanity as two people become a family, and families become a clan, and a clan becomes a tribe, and tribes become nations. [45]

---

[45] Eugene Merrill, Everlasting Dominion: A Theology of the Old Testament. (Nashville, B&H Publishing Group, 2006), 182-3.

This is difficult to grasp as individuals, but in Genesis we are seeing the building blocks of society as individuals influence the nation as a whole, and as we change our understanding of marriage in our culture today we need to understand we are making changes to our nation. [46]

3. What Are The Hurdles?

A. How should someone's faith influence society?

As a follower of Jesus we are called to be salt and light (Matthew 5). We are called to seek justice (Micah 6). We are called to be a blessing and a benefit to those around us, and at the same time Scripture guards the follower of Jesus from pushing biblical values on a people who aren't followers of Jesus (1 Corinthians 5). Therefore, as a follower of Jesus we need to wrestle with what it looks like practically for our faith to influence society. [47]

---

[46] Ryan T. Anderson, Truth Overruled: The Future of Marriage and Religious Freedom, kindle ed., location 302.

[47] Jesus doesn't condemn judgment—only hypocritical judgment. That means there may be room for the Church to retain a prophetic voice on critical issues. There are examples of Biblical figures—and God himself—judging those outside the immediate people of faith (i.e., Israel and the Church):

- God brought judgment on non-Jewish cities because of their widespread acceptance of homosexual conduct. (Gen 19:1-28)
- The Canaanites were morally responsible for sexual sin (Lev 18:6-23)
- In the NT, John the Baptist rebuked Herod Antipas, an Idumean and not part of the people of God, for committing incest with his brother's wife (Mk 6:17-18)
- Paul says Gentiles are violating God's moral standards regarding sexual conduct (Rom 1:26-27)
- "Sexual immorality" is among the reasons that "Babylon" is marked for judgement in God's future (Revelation 18:3, 9)

B. Should the follower of Jesus attend or participate in same-sex marriage?

North Village Church will not host or perform same-sex marriages, but each of us needs to wrestle with how we respond personally to same-sex marriage. There are times when it might be helpful to attend, and there are times when it might be helpful to decline. [48]

C. Does this mean people with homosexual desires who submit those desires to Jesus might not ever get married?

Maybe. First, it is possible that Jesus can change our sexual desires because that's what He does as we mature and grow in Him in all areas of our lives.

Second, it is likely that marriage and children have been too elevated in the local church. We do want to hold marriage in high regard (Hebrews 13), but our purpose in life isn't to get married and have children. Overall, it is likely the local church has placed too much of an emphasis and marriage and children, and we have a lot to learn from followers of Jesus who are setting aside their sexual desires to follow Jesus.

D. Are we being consistent in our convictions on marriage?

Are we being careful not to just isolate same-sex marriage in our attempt to hold marriage in high regard? Are we stewarding the gift of marriage in our own life personally?

---

[48] Should Followers of Jesus Support Same-Sex Marriage?
https://mcleanbible.org/wp-content/uploads/2021/02/Attending-A-Same-Sex-Wedding.pdf

Are we challenging heterosexual couples who are professing faith in Christ and living together before marriage? Are we challenging couples who profess faith in Christ and are quick to get a divorce, remarry, and divorce?

It was Ronald Reagan, as a Governor in California, who implemented "No Fault Divorce" in the 1970's and today divorce is rippling through our country. Therefore, might the follower of Jesus be consistent in their honoring of marriage as a whole? [49]

E. Should there be a distinction between civil unions and biblical marriage?

It's hard to say. It's possible that some might pursue civil unions (not biblical marriage) that are made available to all citizens to have all the privileges of marriage. But the local church is free to officiate biblical marriages, and perhaps that is a common ground that would be helpful.

Remember the Gospel

Overall, lets close with a reminder of why Jesus is so important. It's possible that this conversation on marriage and sexuality is too difficult to explore, and if so, then we would encourage you to set this conversation aside for the moment. At the center of our faith isn't sexual and societal ethics, but at the center of our faith is the life, death and resurrection of Jesus.

Therefore, might we all begin this conversation by leaning into the life of Jesus? Might we read about the life of Jesus?

---

[49] Five Facts About No-Fault Divorce. Joe Carter. August 16, 2019.
https://erlc.com/resource-library/articles/5-facts-about-no-fault-divorce/

Might we look upon the life of Jesus and see the One who created us, knows us, and loves us?

Jesus loves us so much that even when we spit in His face to reject Him, He pursues us to the point of death on a cross and conquers death in the resurrection.

Do you know why Jesus endured the cross? It is because Jesus loves you (Hebrews 12:2). He loves you so much. The invitation of Jesus isn't to get married one day. The invitation of Jesus is that He's already prepared a great wedding day for you (Revelation 19). He has already come to make you pure, dressed in white, ready to be presented at the gates of heaven (Revelation 19).

Might we all start there and hear Jesus inviting us to submit the whole of our life to Him?

Reflective Questions:
1. In this conversation it is easy to fall on one side or the other. What are practical steps you can take to better understand the other perspective?
2. What does it look like for you to honor the gift of marriage in your life personally?

Additional Resources:
- Kevin DeYoung, "What Does the Bible Really Teach About Homosexuality?"
- David Platt, "Compassionate Call to Counter Culture."

What About Transgenderism?

It's possible that some of us are asking the question, "Are we sure we should be addressing this conversation at church? But we're talking about this conversation everywhere else in life.

It is normal to hear teachers in schools having this conversation with our children. People in sports are having this conversation. The legal community is having this conversation. The workplace is having this conversation. Television shows and movies are definitely having this conversation. [50] It would be weird to talk about this conversation in every area of our life, but not in the local church.

---

[50] Transgender Movies and TV Shows. Glamour. March 31, 2021.
https://www.glamour.com/gallery/transgender-movies-and-tv-shows-7-essential-titles-and-where-to-stream-them

Therefore, our hope in this booklet isn't to address this conversation one time so we never have to talk about this conversation again. But we are trying to open up lines of communication to help us engage something we need to engage because the good news of Jesus applies to all areas of life. Therefore, we want to step into this conversation by focusing on three key areas:

1. Where Does Our Culture Land?
2. How Does God's Word Respond?
3. How Do We Respond?

1. Where Does Our Culture Land?

Perhaps some of us remember in a 2015 Vanity Fair that featured the former Olympic Champion Bruce Jenner on their cover with Bruce identifying as a woman, wearing lingerie, and a caption that read, "Call me Caitlyn." [51]

Culturally, it felt like that was the tipping point for our culture in this conversation. It seemed to be the moment the conversation around transgender people began to make its way into our everyday language so that today we seem to be settling on this definition:

> Transgender: Transgender people are those whose gender identity does not match their sex assigned at birth, that they can be trans men, trans women, and also non-binary, meaning they do not identify as men or women.

---

[51] Caitlyn Jenner: The Full Story. Vanity Fair. June 25, 2015. https://www.vanityfair.com/hollywood/2015/06/caitlyn-jenner-bruce-cover-annie-leibovitz

How did our culture land on this definition? Up to this point in history our "gender identity" was determined by the objective fact of our biological sex.

But for many people in our culture today, the facts of biology do not determine your "gender identity" but instead it is your subjective perception of your "gender identity" that ultimately matters. One person put it this way:

"Gender is about what's between your ears, not what's between your legs." [52]

A key term that is used in this conversation today is a term called "Gender Dysphoria:

Gender Dysphoria: Gender dysphoria is a term that describes a sense of unease that a person may have because of a mismatch between their biological sex and their gender identity. [53]

As a result, a person might have considerable psychological and emotional distress about their physical body not matching what they feel they have emotionally, and that creates a state of unhappiness, restlessness and frustration for people with gender dysphoria. [54]

[52] Chaz Bono. Huffington Post. Updated December 6, 2017.
https://www.huffpost.com/entry/chaz-bono-gender-is-betwe_n_363508

[53] Mark D. Yarhouse, Understanding Gender Dysphoria: Navigating Transgender Issues in a Changing Culture. (Downers Grove: IVP Academic, 2015).

[54] Riittakerttu Kaltiala-Heino et al., "Gender Dysphoria in Adolescence: Current Perspectives," Adolescent Health, Medicine, and Therapeutics, 2018; 9: 31–41, doi: 10.2147/AHMT.S135432, Published online at https://www.ncbi.nlm.nih.gov/pmc/articles/PMC5841333/

In addition, it's important to clarify that our culture views this conversation as a conversation of equality, justice, and civil rights for how people are treated.

Our culture believes a person cannot flourish as a person unless they are able to embrace their inner identity, and it's the responsibility of the community at large to accept, affirm, and celebrate their inner identity. [55]

This is why people are genuinely asking in our culture today, "What kind of restrooms need to be made available? What kind of uniforms need to be required? Who can be on which sports team? Which dorm does someone stay in at a youth camp?" And it's likely these questions are only going to increase.

In an attempt to try to simplify this conversation, we've tried to identify two types of people:

- Compassion Perspective: If people experience gender dysphoria, then we should bend toward those people. The conclusion is that male and female categories are just labels, and making these changes are the loving thing to do.

- Congruent Perspective: Generally speaking all of human history has functioned under male and female categories based on biology; therefore, it is disorienting to simply say, "Those things are just labels, and those labels no longer matter."

[55] Supporting Gender Identity. My USF. Amber Hager. 2014.
https://myusf.usfca.edu/caps/supporting-gender-identity

Which perspective do you lean toward? If you are in the Compassion Perspective Group, you would do well to have "compassion" toward those who find this conversation really disorienting.

When people yell, protest and make emotional outbursts to people who disagree, they don't come across as a very loving person. [56]

In addition, if you are in the Congruent Perspective Group you would do well to convey empathy and concern for all people.

Saying things like, "Transgender people are just a fraction of our population" doesn't help because a fraction of a people is still people.

Therefore, we would all do well to identify which group we might be in and then begin to work hard to find common ground with the other group, so that together we can have a healthy conversation with one another.

2. How Does God's Word Respond?

Obviously, the Bible doesn't have the word "transgender" in it, but there is wisdom in Scripture that can speak to how we walk through this conversation today. Let's look at Genesis 1:

> Genesis 1:26-27, "26 Then God said, "Let Us make mankind in Our image, according to Our likeness; and let them rule over the fish of the sea and over the

---

[56] Dave Chappelle fans clash with trans-rights protesters at Netflix rally. New York Post. Alexandra Steigrad. October 20, 2021. https://nypost.com/2021/10/20/dave-chappelle-fans-clash-with-trans-rights-protesters-at-netflix-rally/

birds of the sky and over the livestock and over all the earth, and over every crawling thing that crawls on the earth." 27 So God created man in His own image, in the image of God He created him; male and female He created them."

It's possible that we might see these verses as outdated verses, but these verses teach us about the character of God.

In Genesis 1 we see the God of Scripture is benevolent because He creates us. He is powerful because He speaks creation into existence. He is relational because we are made in His image, and then in verse 27 we see humanity is set apart as "male and female."

Our culture says "male and female" are just social constructs, but we must be careful we aren't overlooking the importance of our physical bodies being made male and female.

The God of Scripture could have identified humanity by our ethnicity (Arab and Egyptian), by our physical height (short and tall), by our weight, by our hair color, but instead the God of Scripture identifies the foundation of humanity as male and female so that early on we see the significance of our physical bodies aligning us with being made in the image of God.

In addition, Scripture places an important emphasis on the intentionality of our physical bodies:

- 1 Corinthians 15:42, "42 So also is the resurrection of the dead. It is sown a perishable **body**, it is raised an imperishable body."

- Psalm 139:13, "For You created my innermost **parts**; You wove me in my mother's womb."
- Romans 8:23, "23 And not only that, but also we ourselves, having the first fruits of the Spirit, even we ourselves groan within ourselves, waiting eagerly for our adoption as sons and daughters, the redemption of our **body**."
- 1 Corinthians 6:19, "19 Or do you not know that your **body** is a temple of the Holy Spirit within you, whom you have from God, and that you are not your own?"

Femininity and masculinity might be a social construct. What we consider feminine, and masculine might change over time based on the culture at the time, but not male and female because in Genesis 1 we are made male and female.

Now, it's possible a person might say, "Genesis-Smenisish. I don't care what Genesis 1 says because this is how I feel."

Fair enough. But we know our feelings and our desires change over time, and we know not all of our feelings and desires are beneficial.

We all have social desires like gossip, slander, bitterness and envy that we shouldn't listen to in life. We all have physical cravings for food that are unhealthy and unhelpful that we shouldn't listen to in life.

Even emotionally we have to be careful that we don't ruminate on some feelings and desires around anxiety, depression, or isolation that we shouldn't listen to in life.

The gospel is that Jesus has come, God in the flesh, to expose the brokenness of our soul all the way down to our feelings and desires and call us turn to Jesus and find life in Jesus, and that includes our sexual desires.

Again, it's possible that we still want to push back on this conversation and say to ourselves, "And we're basing all of this on some verses in the Old Testament?" Really?

Yes, we have this view toward our sexual desires and physical body because Jesus based His conclusions on sexual desires from the Old Testament.

In Matthew 19 Jesus is speaking about divorce and marriage, and in that moment, Jesus is talking about the sexuality of the day. But Jesus doesn't say, "I love you, you do what feels right."

No, Jesus quotes Genesis 1 and 2 and references humanity being made male and female, becoming one flesh in marriage, so that these verses aren't just old verses, but foundational verses that shape all of life.

3. How Do We Respond?

A. God's Word speaks into our mind and our bodies.

It's possible that today we have elevated our mind and emotions over our bodies, but God's Word speaks over both.

If a person battled bulimia, we would see someone who outwardly displays a physical body that is thing. But inwardly they believe they are grossly overweight. As a result, this person would build up an unhealthy pattern of expelling their food to help them match the outside of their body to the inside of how they feel.

In that moment we wouldn't want to say to them, "You should listen to how you feel." They would be completely sincere in how they felt, but they would be objectively wrong. So that as a follower of Jesus our final authority in life isn't our bodies or our minds or our emotions, but God's Word speaks into our body, mind and emotions.

B. God's Word teaches the follower of Jesus to lead out in these conversations with humility and compassion.

When we talk to people who disagree with us, or people who agree with us, we must lead out with humility. The gospel is that we are all broken people in need of a Savior, therefore, our tone with ourselves and others should drip with compassion.

All people might not all be able to relate to gender dysphoria, but every follower of Jesus knows what it is like to have levels and layers of discomfort with their bodies.

We know what it is like to live with failing bodies. We know what it is like to wish our bodies looked different on some level, therefore, might our words and tone drip with compassion.

Proverbs 18:13, "If one gives an answer before he hears it is our folly and shame." Therefore, might we be slow to speak and quick to listen because we're not going to speak well if we aren't listening well.

Might we ask people, "If you're comfortable, will you share more about your experiences?" Might we learn from one another? The people around us might be battered and bruised from the challenges of life, and in Jesus we have a Savior who is gentle with our bruises.

C. God's Word speaks to how we should respond in practical conversations.

It is likely that many of us are engaging the conversation around preferred pronouns, and we all have a myriad of feelings on this subject, but let us consider God's Word:

> Proverbs 26:4, "Do not answer a fool according to his foolishness, or you will also be like him."

> Proverbs 26:5, "Answer a fool as his foolishness deserves, so that he will not be wise in his own eyes."

Isn't that helpful? Do we or don't we, and God's Word says, "yes." There is wisdom in sometimes answering people in their non-biblical assumptions because sometimes-running with that concept-we can show them how it might fall apart.

If a person asks us to address them by a certain name or a certain pronoun, and it helps us further the relationship so that we might more fully show them Jesus, then absolutely we should give ground on something as simple as a name or a pronoun.

But, if there is a committed partner in our church family who has expressed faith in Jesus, maturing in Jesus, and then one day asks us to address them with a different name or a different pronoun, then in that instance it would be best to not answer them according to their folly because we would be affirming their folly.

In the end, if you are a person who is walking through gender dysphoria, going by preferred pronouns, or living as a transgender man or woman, then please know you are always welcome here at North Village Church.

In no way will we mock or belittle someone as we walk through these conversations, but we invite you here, welcome you here, and want you here, so that we might all gather to be reminded of the living hope we have in Jesus.

It was Jesus who approached the blind, deaf and hurting, and people would ask, "Is the pain and brokenness the result of their sin, or their parent's sin?" (John 9) The people wanted to know the purpose for the pain. The people wanted to know who to blame.

Jesus answered, and said, ""It was neither that this man sinned, nor his parents; but it was so that the works of God might be displayed in him."

This isn't Jesus denying sin, or Genesis 3, but Jesus is lifting our eyes to see that we can turn to Him with all of our pain at every level and find hope in Him.

It's not by sidestepping the pain, blocking out the pain, ignoring the pain, or renaming the pain, but turning to Him with our pain.

We want to turn to the One who experienced the greatest pain we could ever imagine at the cross, and the One who says there is pain now, but one day that pain will be completely removed. Might we all turn to Him!

Reflective Questions:
1. In this conversation it is easy to fall on one side or the other. What are practical steps you can take to better understand the other perspective?
2. What does it look like for you personally to engage this conversation today?

Additional Resources:
- Transexuality and Ordination by Robert Gagnon.
- Understanding Gender Dysphoria by Mark Yarhouse.

Growing In Discernment

What exactly is discernment? How does discernment relate to spiritual growth, and all the conversations that are taking place around us today?

God's Word speaks to the importance of His people being able to navigate our culture wisely. Here are a few scriptures that teach us about the importance of discernment:

- 1 Thessalonians 5:21-22, "21 But examine everything carefully; hold fast to that which is good; 22 abstain from every form of evil."
- 1 John 3:26, "26 These things I have written to you concerning those who are trying to deceive you."
- 1 Peter 5:8-9, "8 Be of sober spirit, be on the alert. Your adversary, the devil, prowls around like a

roaring lion, seeking someone to devour. 9 But resist him, firm in your faith, knowing that the same experiences of suffering are being accomplished by your brethren who are in the world."

Sometimes we are uncomfortable with discernment because it might feel like we are judging others, and Jesus teaches us not to judge (Matthew 7:1).

But the discernment we are talking about isn't showing partiality toward others based on outward appearances. Instead, we are "examining, analyzing, and trying" to determine what is true and godly, and what is false and ungodly. Below are a few principles that have proven to be helpful as we continue to grow and mature in our faith:

Rhetorical Context: Rhetorical Context refers to the circumstances surrounding an act of reading or composition, therefore, when we talk about historical events in Scripture, or in life, we need to remember the historical context of when those events were taking place. Who is the primary agent? Who is the audience? What do we know about the context of culture of that day? How was the event presented?

Experiential Authority: There is a narrative in our culture today that we have to experience something to talk about something.

For example, our culture might conclude a white person can't talk about racism because our country exists in a white dominant culture. Or a man can't talk about what it is like to be a woman because he isn't a woman.

There is *some* merit to that narrative, and there are things that we can / can't learn from one another because of our experiences, but if we take that logic to it's fullest measure then we just end up in segregated circles unable to learn from one another.

In addition, our experiences, although valid, are not a reliable authority for us to make foundational decisions in our life. We want to be aware of our experiences, but ultimately submit our experiences to God's Word.

Cherry Picking: It is really common right now for people to pick 3-5 events on a historical timeline that might be true, and then make a Tik-Tok video and flash those 3-5 events on the screen and say, "See...Gotcha!"

But we need to look at the whole of Scripture or the historical event to understand a wider description of what actually took place.

The Other Side: It is fairly common these days for articles, news, social media, etc. to only present one side of the argument, but we would do well to consider the other side.

The temptation is to dismiss the other side of the argument as stupid, foolish, unbiblical, and dangerous. But these conversations we are having today are incredibly complex and we would do well to present a posture of humility as we try to understand the other perspective.

Grace / Truth: It is fairly common for people to fall on either a side of grace or a side of truth. It's almost a personality trait!

Some people seem to be layered in compassion, mercy, empathy, being generous (Grace), and some people seem to be layered in justice, rules, law, order (Truth).

Therefore, we would do well to identify which one we tend to lean toward, and then we would do well to be mindful of who we are talking to at the moment.

If someone layered in (Truth) is talking about a conversation with justice, rules, law, and order and they happen to be talking to someone who is layered in (Grace), then these two people are going to talk past each other, often vilifying one another, and yet both grace and truth are biblical concepts we can't pit against one another.

Claiming Faith Is Dangerous: In the recent past we have seen extremist groups create pockets of danger around the world. Therefore, our culture is trying to neutralize faith in general with statements like "all faiths are basically the same."

First, the statement, "All faiths are basically the same" is incredibly offensive, and for a culture that values tolerance, it is surprisingly overlooked.

Second, that statement is arrogant because it is an "all" encompassing statement that tries to present itself as wise and generous. It is true that some groups have drifted toward dangerous behavior, but it is also true that non-religious groups have drifted toward dangerous behavior.

Someone or Something Is Trying To Persuade Us All The Time: When you watch movies, listen to music, look at fashion, follow politics, listen to a sermon, watch YouTube, there is a message, and the intent of the message is to persuade. Therefore, might we resist the temptation to "check out" and instead always be on the alert by asking, "What is the message?"

What are they trying to make me feel? What are they trying to make me believe? Who is the authority? Is the authority reliable?

Sex Is Just Physical: As a culture we have philosophically separated our bodies to be independent objects so that the narrative in our culture today is that sex is just physical.

Our bodies are created in the image of God, and our bodies absolutely influence our mind, emotions and relationships, therefore, we would do well to be on guard as to how this type of thinking might influence us today.

Closing -

In the end, the best action we can take to grow in discernment is to believe in Jesus. When we confess with our mouth that Jesus is Lord, and believe in our heart that He conquered death, we are indwelled with the Holy Spirit. The Holy Spirit is our teacher in all things!

In addition, we want to commit to a local church and begin to grow in our understanding of Scripture.   We want to learn how to read Scripture. We want to learn how to study Scripture. We want to grow in our enjoyment of obeying Scripture. We want to learn how to share God's Word with others.

As we are indwelled with the Holy Spirit, equipped with God's Word, and engaged with God's people, we might have moments in life where we lack discernment and stumble into deception, but we can be confident that the Lord will use those moments to draw us back to Himself and strengthen our faith in Him.

Made in the USA
Coppell, TX
06 March 2022